Studying Interpersonal Communication

About this series...

Series Editors: Mark L. Knapp & John A. Daly,
both at the University of Texas

Designed for college and university undergraduates, the **Interpersonal Commtexts** series will also interest a much larger general audience. Ideal as basic or supplementary texts, these volumes are suited for courses in the development and practice of interpersonal skills; verbal and nonverbal behavior (the basis of interpersonal transactions); functions of communication in face-to-face interaction; the development of interpersonal behavior at various points in the lifespan; and intergroup and intercultural aspects of interpersonal communication. Readable and comprehensive, the **Interpersonal Commtexts** describe contexts within which interpersonal communication takes place and provide ways to study and understand the interpersonal communication process.

In this series...

1 **EVERYDAY CONVERSATION**
by Robert E. Nofsinger

2 **STUDYING INTERPERSONAL COMMUNICATION**
The Research Experience
by Ruth Anne Clark

3 **BRIDGING DIFFERENCES**
Effective Intergroup Communication
by William B. Gudykunst

Studying
Interpersonal
Communication
The Research Experience

Ruth Anne Clark

INTERPERSONAL COMMTEXTS 2

SAGE PUBLICATIONS
The International Professional Publishers
Newbury Park   London   New Delhi

For information address:

SAGE Publications, Inc.
2455 Teller Road
Newbury Park, California 91320

SAGE Publications Ltd.
6 Bonhill Street
London EC2A 4PU
England

SAGE Publications India Pvt. Ltd.
M-32 Market
Greater Kailash I
New Delhi 110 048 India

Printed in the United States of America

Library of Congress Cataloging-in-Publication Data

Clark, Ruth Anne.
　　Studying interpersonal communication : the research experience / by Ruth Anne Clark.
　　　　p.　　cm. — (Interpersonal commtexts ; v. 2)
　　Includes bibliographical references and index.
　　ISBN 0-8039-3305-3. — ISBN 0-8039-3306-1 (pbk.)
　　1. Interpersonal communication—Research—Methodology. I. Title.
II. Series.
　　BF637.C45C53　1991
　　302.2'0724—dc20　　　　　　　　　　　　　　　　　　　　90-24233
　　　　　　　　　　　　　　　　　　　　　　　　　　　　　　　　　CIP

FIRST PRINTING, 1991

Sage Production Editor: Astrid Virding

Contents

Preface

Do you ever draw generalizations about interpersonal communication based on your observations? For instance, you might conclude that members of one sorority are more supportive of each other than members of another sorority. Or you might decide that individuals who talk a lot at a party are more popular than other individuals. Or you might infer that individuals who make grammatical blunders are judged to be inept.

Most of the time, however, both our observations and inferences are casual rather than systematic. Since we do not have a carefully selected sample of behavior, we rely on whatever information may be available. Rather than explicitly defining our terms, we settle for a general notion of key concepts such as "supportive," "popular," or "inept." Moreover, because we have no real measures of these concepts, we rely on our own judgments of what it means to be supportive, popular, or inept. And so on. The difficulty, then, is that our inferences may lack precision, may not be persuasive to others, and worst of all, may simply be wrong.

If we wish to study interpersonal communication, therefore, it is important to understand systematic procedures that yield inferences that we can have faith in and that others will be willing to accept. And that is what this book is about, the systematic empirical study of interpersonal communication. Learning to study interpersonal communication in this manner does not require special abilities or background. Certainly you do not need to know advanced mathematics. The empirical study of interpersonal communication is like all scientific inquiry: It requires clear thinking.

The student encountering the terminology of experimental and descriptive methods for the first time may initially feel burdened by the need to master a new vocabulary. This vocabulary is not large, however. It contains perhaps 20 new terms. As you read this book, you will encounter many of these terms in the first chapter. Don't try to memorize them: simply try to understand them. As they are repeated throughout the remainder of the text, hopefully they will come to be terms that you can understand and use with ease.

The emphasis in this book is on experimental methodology. This is not because experimental methodology is of more value than descriptive approaches. (The distinction between these two types of research is made in Chapter 1). Rather, this emphasis was selected because the study of experimental methodology introduces core concepts in a systematic way that is useful in conceptualizing any piece of empirical research.

The purpose of this book is to help you become critical consumers of the empirical research in interpersonal communication. Moreover, by the time you have finished the book, you may want to design a simple study yourself. Although you will not have the technical tools for careful measurement and statistical analysis, you will have acquired a manner of thinking critically about research questions that should enable you to design a study. You may discover that conducting your first empirical research is one of the most exhilarating experiences you have as a student. It is exciting to realize that you can go beyond understanding the research of others to having the potential to make a personal contribution to a body of thought.

The Nature of
Communication Research

As students of interpersonal communication, imagine that you are interested in the following question: Is the satisfaction of marital partners with the marriage directly related to the amount of communication between the partners? You observe couples you come into contact with, try to judge how much they communicate with each other in general, and then estimate their level of satisfaction with the marriage. We make such casual inferences frequently.

But our conclusions may be inaccurate. The couples you encountered may not have been typical of most marital partners. Your assessment of the amount of communication between the partners may have been biased by the circumstances in which you encountered them. And your estimate of their satisfaction with the marriage may have been faulty because you were able to observe them only when they were on their best public behavior. In short, you just don't know how accurate your answer to the question is.

❏ Why Understand the Research Process

RESEARCH ENHANCES THE ACCURACY OF OUR INFERENCES

In the example above, we might have carefully measured both the amount of communication between marital partners and their degree of satisfaction with the marriage. We might also have taken into account other factors that could affect the partners' level of satisfaction (such as length of marriage and outside sources of stress). By using such procedures we would be more confident about the relationship observed between the amount of communication and marital satisfaction. One of the most important reasons for conducting research is that we want to be accurate about the conclusions we draw.

As we shall see later, the results of a single research project are never completely conclusive. That is, on the basis of a single study, we could not conclude that marital satisfaction is always related to the amount of communication shared by the couple. Therefore it is important to understand the research process in order to be able to evaluate investigations in the same area that seem to present conflicting results.

Such circumstances are encountered frequently in medical research. For instance, women must decide whether they increase their risk of incurring breast cancer if they take birth control pills when the evidence is conflicting. The more we understand the research process, the better able we are to compare and evaluate specific studies.

In interpersonal communication we also find conflicting evidence. For instance, Shaffer and Ogden (1986) note that most research indicates that women engage in more self disclosure than men; yet this is not always the case. Understanding the research process helps us to determine whether some of the work reported is faulty, or whether we can identify specific circumstances in which men are likely to defy the general pattern.

RESEARCH ENABLES US TO MAKE PREDICTIONS

If we feel confident in our conclusions regarding the relationships among variables, then we can make predictions in specific cases. For example, suppose we find that the amount of communication among marital partners is associated with more satisfaction with the marriage. We could then look at specific marital partners and, if we could assess the amount of communication between them, make predictions about the general level of satisfaction they experience with the marriage. It might be possible to extend this line of work to couples prior to their marriage, which then would enable us to predict level of satisfaction with the marriage before it even occurs. Needless to say, this could be quite useful.

RESEARCH ENABLES US TO INTERVENE TO ALTER OUTCOMES

If we have faith in conclusions reached by careful research, we can go beyond making predictions to actually intervening to alter outcomes. Suppose we encounter a couple who is experiencing dissatisfaction with their marriage and we have evidence that they communicate very little with each other. A counselor might then suggest to the couple that they try to increase their communication with each other, since there is reason to believe that amount of communication is associated with marital satisfaction. Thus research can serve as the basis of intervening in situations to produce more desirable outcomes. As you can see, then, understanding the research process is important not only for those who intend to conduct research projects, but for all of us who need to use the findings of research as well.

❏ Basic Concepts in Empirical Research

As we saw earlier, casual observations can produce misleading conclusions. Therefore, researchers engage in systematic
direct observation of phenomena of interest, which is called
empirical research. Rather than relying on observations reported
by others, even very reputable observations, empirical research
is based on firsthand observation. Moreover, the observations
are not casual or random, but are systematic (i.e., observations
are made under carefully predetermined conditions).

A researcher could systematically observe almost any phenomenon. For instance, one could observe which presidential
candidate speaks in shorter words. But the kind of phenomena
that are of interest to us transcend specific situations. We shall
focus on the relationship between two or more variables. A
variable is simply a class of phenomena that differs from each
other along some specific dimension. Both marital satisfaction
and amount of communication with spouse are variables. There
are different or varying levels of satisfaction and different or
varying amounts of communication with spouse.

Thus when we ask whether the amount of communication
between spouses is related to the level of satisfaction with the
marriage, we are studying the relationship between two variables. The reason we are interested in studying relationships
between variables is because it allows us to make specific predictions and at times even to alter outcomes.

The statements or propositions that describe the anticipated
relationships among variables are called hypotheses or research
questions. *Hypotheses* describe predicted relationships among
variables. *Research questions* pose questions about potential relationships among variables. Thus the researcher might hypothesize that "the more marital partners communicate with
each other, the greater the level of their marital satisfaction."
A research question addressing the same issue might be stated:
"Is the level of marital satisfaction related to the amount
of communication among marital partners?" Typically the
researcher uses a hypothesis when there is sufficient evidence

to make a specific prediction about the relationship expected between the variables. Regardless of whether a hypothesis or a research question is pursued, the purpose of the kind of research in which we are interested is to find recurring and predictable relationships among variables.

A crucial feature of good research is that it takes account of potentially contaminating variables. *Potentially contaminating variables* are variables other than those being investigated that can obscure the real relationship among the variables under investigation. For instance, if the researcher studied only couples who had been married less than six months, the researcher might conclude that there is no relationship between the amount of communication between marital partners and satisfaction with the marriage. In this case, length of marriage might be a potentially contaminating variable. Perhaps newlyweds are excited enough about marriage to overlook difficulties that individuals married for many years do not. In such a situation, failure to take account of length of marriage might lead to a generalization that is not true for couples who have been married longer. We shall see later that a variety of approaches are available to the researcher for dealing with such potentially contaminating variables. But such variables must be dealt with if the conclusions drawn are to be generalizable to a variety of situations.

❏ Types of Research

We will be discussing two major types of empirical research, experimental and descriptive.

EXPERIMENTAL RESEARCH

Experimental research is research in which one or more variables is manipulated under controlled conditions in order to observe the impact on another variable of interest. The crucial distinction between experimental and descriptive research is that in experimental studies at least one variable is manipulated under controlled conditions while in descriptive studies the way that the variables are related is observed without intervention.

Independent Variable

An experimental study involves at least two variables, an independent and a dependent variable. The *independent variable* is the variable the experimenter manipulates in order to observe its impact on the dependent variable. Put another way, the independent variable is deliberately manipulated; then the dependent variable is assessed to determine the influence of the manipulation.

Consider again the question of whether amount of communication between marital partners is related to the degree of satisfaction with the relationship. It is possible to study this question experimentally. The researcher might treat amount of communication as an independent variable. If so, the researcher would deliberately manipulate the amount of communication between marital partners. For instance, the researcher might randomly divide a large number of married couples into three groups. With one group, the researcher might ask each couple to attempt to talk with each other more frequently than usual. Another group might be asked to talk with each other less frequently than usual. The third group would be asked to talk about as frequently as they normally do. After a specified period of time, perhaps three months, the researcher might measure the level of marital satisfaction of all the couples and compare the average level of satisfaction for the three groups.

In any experiment, there must be at least two levels or conditions of the independent variable. In our example, there were three levels of communication: more than usual, less than usual, and usual amount of time. As you can see, the *levels or conditions of an independent variable* are the specific embodiments of the independent variable.

Dependent Variable

The *dependent variable* is the variable that has the potential to fluctuate as a result of the manipulation of the independent variable. In our example, then, the dependent variable is level of marital satisfaction.

Some studies involve more than one dependent variable. Each dependent variable helps constitute a separate research question or hypothesis. In our example, the researcher might choose to assess more than satisfaction with the marriage. For instance, the researcher might also assess how well the marital partners know the preferences of their mates. This second dependent variable would help form a new research question: Is amount of communication between marital partners related to how well the partners know their mates' preferences?

Experimental Unit

Another essential ingredient of a research design is the experimental unit. An *experimental unit* is the person or object embodying the dependent variable. Marital satisfaction does not exist in isolation; it exists in people. Thus in our sample study, the experimental units are the people whose level of satisfaction with their marriages is being monitored. When the experimental units are humans or other living beings, they are called *subjects* (frequently abbreviated as Ss) or participants or respondents.

Not all experimental units are living beings. In agricultural research, for instance, the experimental unit might be plots of ground. In communication research, however, the experimental unit typically is a human subject. As we shall see later, the experimenter must exert care in the selection of the subjects and in their assignment to the various conditions of the independent variable to avoid introducing contaminating variables to the design of the study. In an experiment, subjects should be assigned randomly to the various conditions of the independent variable.

Potentially Contaminating Variables

As mentioned earlier, if the conclusion of the research is to be generalizable, the design (i.e., the way the experiment is set up) must deal with potentially contaminating variables. *Potentially contaminating variables* are variables other than the independent variable(s) that may influence the dependent variable. Put another way, potentially contaminating variables (also called confounding variables) may obscure the true relationship between the independent and the dependent variables by influencing some conditions of the independent variable more than others.

Consider again out experimental design in which the researcher was manipulating the amount of communication between marital partners. Suppose that the researcher has asked for volunteers for each of the three groups. It is possible that couples who were very happy with their marriages would have volunteered for the group asked to increase the amount of their communication. Similarly, couples who were unhappy with their marriages might volunteer for the group asked to decrease their communication.

If the researcher then compared the average level of marital satisfaction of the three groups at the end of three months, it would not be surprising to find that the group that increased communication was more satisfied than the group that decreased communication. But we could not be sure of what was responsible for the different levels of satisfaction of the two groups. The one group was already more satisfied with their marriages than the other group before any alterations were made in communication. In this case we would call initial level of satisfaction a contaminating or confounding variable because it obscures our ability to tell whether altering amount of communication changes the level of satisfaction of marital partners. Later we will examine options available to the re-searcher for avoiding the problem of contaminating variables.

Operational Definitions

Earlier we said that the researcher assesses the impact of the manipulation of the independent variable on the dependent variable. This statement is not quite accurate. This impact cannot be measured directly. Rather, the researcher must use operational definitions of both the independent and dependent variables that reflect the conceptual definitions of these variables.

An *operational definition* is a set of procedures for either producing or identifying specific conditions of a variable under investigation. An operational definition enables the researcher to translate an abstract concept (e.g., marital satisfaction or attitude change) into an observable phenomenon.

Operational definitions of the independent variable typically are a set of instructions or procedures for producing the conditions of the variable to be investigated. Amount of communication between marital partners cannot be manipulated directly. The researcher has no means of actually controlling the amount of communication between two people. But there are a variety of ways in which the researcher can attempt to influence the amount of communication between marital partners. In our sample study, the operational definition for manipulating the amount of communication between marital partners was simply a request from the researcher to communicate more, or less, or the same as usual.

Other procedures might have been used to manipulate the independent variable of amount of communication. For example, the researcher might have identified specific times when subjects in one group would be asked to be sure to communicate with each other while subjects in another group would be asked to refrain from communicating. Or the researcher might have offered a reward to one group if subjects could verify (perhaps with tape recordings) that they had increased their communication. Similarly, subjects in another group would have been rewarded for decreasing their communication.

The procedures available to the researcher for manipulating the independent variable differ depending on the nature of the variable, but there are always multiple options.

The operational definition of the dependent variable typically is a set of procedures for identifying changes in the value of the dependent variable. With the dependent variable, the task is not to *produce* conditions of the variable as it was with the independent variable, but rather to *identify or assess* variations in the dependent variable produced by manipulation of the independent variable. In other words, the operational definition of a dependent variable typically is a means for measuring or assessing fluctuation in the dependent variable produced by the manipulation of the independent variable.

Thus in our sample study, the operational definition of marital satisfaction would be an instrument designed to measure the degree of marital satisfaction. As with the independent variable, the researcher is likely to have several options from which to select an operational definition of the dependent variable. Later we will discuss the attributes of a good dependent measure that guide this selection.

DESCRIPTIVE RESEARCH

Descriptive research differs from experimental work in one fundamental respect: Variables are not manipulated but rather are observed as they naturally occur. *Descriptive research*, then, can be defined as research in which relationships among variables are observed as they occur naturally (without intervention or manipulation).

Since no variable is manipulated, in descriptive research we do not label one variable as an independent variable and another as dependent. At times, however, we may think of one variable as the predictor and the other as the criterion or predicted variable. Consider again the relationship between the

amount of communication and marital satisfaction. We may
think of the amount of communication as the predictor variable
and the degree of satisfaction as the cri-
terion or predicted variable.

One limitation of descriptive research
is that we cannot make statements of
causation. We cannot say that more
communication leads to or produces
greater marital satisfaction. In reality,
greater satisfaction with the marriage
might produce more communication,
which might in turn lead to even greater
satisfaction.

One danger in descriptive research is that other variables may confound the relationship under investigation.

Descriptive studies share many fea-
tures with experimental studies. In descriptive research there
is always an experimental unit, typically a human subject or
participant in interpersonal communication research. And
again the researcher must take account of potentially contaminating variables.

Since there is no independent variable, however, no variable
is manipulated in descriptive research. The operational definitions of all variables in descriptive research are procedures for
identifying or assessing fluctuations in the variables. Suppose
that we decided to pursue our question about the relationship
of amount of communication and marital satisfaction using a
descriptive design. Rather than attempting to manipulate the
amount of communication, we would attempt to assess the
amount of communication within couples *as it occurs naturally.*
We would also, of course, assess the level of marital satisfaction
within couples.

COMPARISON OF EXPERIMENTAL AND
DESCRIPTIVE RESEARCH

One major danger in descriptive research is that variables
other than those being investigated may confound the relationship under investigation (i.e., be contaminating or confounding

variables). Suppose that we conduct a descriptive study and discover that the greater the amount of communication that couples share, the greater their level of satisfaction with the marriage. Before we conclude that considerable communication is an essential factor in marital satisfaction, we might look for other variables that could help explain this relationship. We might discover, for instance, that the same couples who communicate extensively engage in more shared activities than other couples. Then we are no longer certain whether it is the communication or shared activities that is most strongly related to marital satisfaction. Fortunately there are methods for disentangling such issues if we are able to measure all the variables involved. But as you can see, descriptive studies may involve confounding variables.

By contrast, descriptive study frequently is superior to experimental study on terms of representing real differences in the variable designated as the independent one in an experimental study. Recall that in our sample study the operational definition of the independent variable was a request for groups to communicate either more frequently, less frequently, or as usual. Even if couples faithfully executed this request, we cannot be sure that the difference in their communication approximated natural communication. Those instructed to communicate more may have struggled to find things to discuss that they didn't have any real desire to talk about. And those instructed to talk less may have found it difficult to engage in their normal routines. So the biggest pitfall of experimental research typically is finding realistic manipulations of the independent variable.

The greatest advantage of the experimental study, however, is that the independent variable can be isolated from others that it is naturally closely associated with (considerable communication being associated with shared activities, for instance). Thus when we find that the independent variable does produce differences in the dependent variable, we have a better basis of inferring causality than we do with descriptive studies. If we wanted to actually produce differences in the dependent variable, we would have some notion of how to do this. Suppose that in an experimental study we did find that couples instructed to communicate more were found three months later to be more satisfied with their marriages than those instructed to communicate as usual or less frequently than normal. We then would have grounds for recommending more communication to couples desiring to improve their marital relationship. In some cases the researcher does not have the option of choosing between a descriptive and an experimental design. Some variables cannot or should not be manipulated. Sex, age, and political affiliation are examples of such variables. Frequently, however, the researcher is faced with a choice between conducting an experiment and a descriptive study. In such cases the researcher needs to consider the advantages and limitations of the two types of designs to determine which option better serves the rationale for conducting the study.

❏ Decisions in Research

Sometimes people think of empirical research as being much like mathematics: There is one appropriate way to proceed with a research project, and if the researcher is careful, the right conclusion will be reached. This, however, is not the case in designing research projects. Any research question or hypothesis can be pursued in an infinite number of ways. The research enterprise involves a series of decisions or choices, each of which can affect the outcome. Each option selected will have specific advantages, but may also have specific limitations. Thus designing a study requires a great deal of judgment from the researcher, with the decisions always being guided by the researcher's rationale or motivation for pursuing the question or hypothesis. The ultimate criterion for making all decisions in designing the project is what will yield the most useful information for the researcher's purpose.

In the following section we preview the major decisions confronting the researcher. In later chapters we will discuss the options available at each stage of decision and the factors that guide the choices to be made.

EVALUATING THE SIGNIFICANCE OF
THE RESEARCH QUESTION

The first decision confronting the researcher is whether to go forward with the project. Since the researcher's time is finite, it is necessary to select projects that genuinely are worth the investment of time. It is tempting to engage in a study simply because it is interesting or because it would be an obvious advance over one already completed. But before plunging ahead with any project, the researcher should ask two questions. First, is the general area worth an investment of time? Second, does the particular study under consideration make a unique and important contribution to the general area? Only when both questions are answered affirmatively should the researcher proceed.

REFINING CONCEPTUAL DEFINITIONS

The researcher also should not proceed before reaching a clear understanding of what is to be studied. It is easy to think in global terms about variables such as marital satisfaction, communication apprehension, or ego involvement. It is much more difficult to define such terms with enough precision to engage in a research project. For example, communication apprehension may refer to the amount of anxiety an individual reports feeling while communicating, or to the amount of anxiety others perceive that the individual is experiencing, or to the amount of anxiety evidenced in physiological measures. Although these three concepts of communication apprehension are related, they are not synonymous. Thus before any attempt is made to operationally define the variables to be investigated, the researcher must decide precisely what is meant conceptually by each variable.

CHOOSING BETWEEN AN EXPERIMENTAL AND DESCRIPTIVE STUDY

The next major decision is whether to rely on an experimental or descriptive approach. Beyond the general considerations outlined earlier, an important determinant of which approach to use is the utility of operational definitions available within each approach. As you might expect, the decisions involved in designing a study frequently are interlocked.

SELECTING OPERATIONAL DEFINITIONS OF THE VARIABLE

As we discussed earlier, the researcher cannot observe directly abstract concepts. They first must be translated into observable phenomena by means of operational definitions. As we noted, there are many operational definitions that the researcher could use for any given concept. Consequently, a crucial set of decisions in designing a study involves the selection of the operational definitions for each of the conceptual variables.

SELECTING THE SPECIFIC CONTEXT FOR THE STUDY

Suppose that the individual variable requires manipulation of some feature of a message (level of self disclosure, for instance). Then a significant factor in the outcome of the study is the nature of the basic message in which the manipulation is embedded. One can imagine that reactions to self disclosure would be different if they occurred as part of a casual conversation with a friend or as part of an initial conversation with a stranger. Consequently, the researcher must consider carefully the impact of the context in which the variables are embedded. Once again the researcher should be guided in the selection of context by the rationale underlying the research question or hypothesis.

❏ Selecting and Allocating Subjects

The researcher must select or gain access to the individuals who will serve as subjects or participants in the study. The kinds of individuals who function as participants also may significantly affect the results. For instance, the relationship between amount of communication and marital satisfaction may vary with different groups of individuals. Age, social class, and ethnic background are factors that might influence expectations of the role of communication in marriage.

Similarly, the researcher must assign subjects to specific treatment conditions in an experimental design. Recall the manipulation of amount of communication of marital partners, instructing different groups to communicate more, less, or do the same amount as usual. Clearly it would be important that the groups do not differ in their initial levels of satisfaction or amount of communication. For this reason, random assignment of subjects to experimental conditions is the most common way of allocating subjects.

CODING DATA

Once the data are gathered and the experimenter begins to apply the operational definition of the dependent variable, it may be necessary to make additional decisions. If the subjects' responses are already in scaled form (responses to a standard attitude scale, for instance), the decisions typically are relatively trivial. For example, the researcher might need to decide what to do when a respondent failed to complete one of a series of scales.

If the subjects' responses are relatively open-ended and must be coded into categories, the decisions regarding how to code particular responses frequently are of great importance. Suppose, for example, that the subjects produced persuasive messages, and the dependent variable is the number of different types of persuasive appeals used. If the category system being used contains twenty different types of appeals, categorizing some responses may be quite difficult and therefore could affect the conclusions reached.

ANALYZING DATA

The statistical procedures selected to analyze the data will influence the outcome of the study. Selecting alternative analyses typically will not lead to conflicting results. However, the method of analysis will determine how much information is extracted from the data and, more important, what the particular focus of the results will be. For instance, depending on the statistical analysis selected, emphasis may be placed on individual differences in behavior or on the elements of behavior that tend to be relatively stable across individuals with respect to the variable under consideration.

REPORTING THE STUDY

As is the case with analysis of data, the choices the researcher makes in reporting the study can sharply alter the reader's interpretation of the results. Again, the alternative ways in which the study might be reported do not lead to conflicting outcomes, but to very different emphases. For example, at times the same set of data may be tied to different theoretical bodies of literature. The focus in reporting a study can influence, to a very great extent, the readers' interpretation of the project.

❑ Preview

Before elaborating on the kinds of choices outlined above, it is useful to understand the attributes of good research. If you know what constitutes good research, then you have a set of criteria for evaluating the options that are available at each point of decision making. Consequently, the next section of the book is devoted to identifying the three primary attributes of good research. The first of these concerns the quality of the research question or hypothesis itself. The second is called internal validity, and refers to the quality of the internal logic of the design. The third is labeled external validity and is concerned with the generalizability of the results.

The remaining chapters then elaborate the major kinds of decisions faced by the researcher. Chapter 5 discusses decisions related to the independent variable. Chapter 6 deals with treatment of subjects. Chapters 7 and 8 concentrate on issues surrounding the dependent variable. Chapters 9, 10, and 11 describe the statistical treatment of the data, and Chapter 12 describes concerns in reporting the study.

❑ Study Questions

Consider this research question: During the initial interaction among strangers, which approach generates more liking for person A: disclosing personal information or encouraging the other to talk about his or her interests? Divide into groups of four and answer the following questions.

1. Can the question be reworded as a hypothesis?
2. Suppose you wanted to pursue the question as a descriptive study. What would be the predictor value? What would be the criterion variable?
3. If you wanted to pursue the question as an experiment, what would be the independent variable? The dependent variable?
4. Suggest a manipulation for the independent variable.
5. What potentially contaminating variables might you be concerned with?
6. What general kind of operational definition of the dependent variable might you use?

2

Evaluation of the Research Question

The first criterion for evaluating any research project is the value of the research question itself. It can be argued that there is potential merit in any project. However, as mentioned earlier, the time of the researcher is finite. Moreover, outlets for reporting research (journals, monographs, books, etc.) are limited as well. Consequently it seems sensible to ask first whether a research question or hypothesis is worth pursuing.

Three criteria are useful in assessing the value of the question to be pursued. First, the question or hypothesis should be clear and precise. Second, the question should be amenable to study. It should lend itself to a design that has all the attributes essential to good research. And finally, the question itself should be of significance. None of these criteria is easy to apply. The significance of the question, in fact, is particularly difficult to evaluate. We shall suggest some guidelines, however, that we hope will be useful in making the judgments necessary.

❏ Clarity and Precision of the Question

When the project is completed, it is important that both the researcher and consumer understand what has been learned. Clarity and precision of the question and conclusions are a function of a number of factors, the most common of which are described below.

CONCEPTUAL CLARITY OF THE VARIABLES

The variables embedded in the research questions must have clear conceptual definitions before any attempt is made to operationalize them. Suppose that the hypothesis is that individuals who are highly ego involved in an issue will exhibit greater participation in a group discussion than individuals who are less ego involved. The definitions of both ego involvement and participation are problematic. Consider the alternative conceptions of ego involvement that might be implied by the hypothesis. Ego involvement might refer to the extent of consequences the issue holds for the individual. However, ego involvement could also mean the extent to which an individual would make sacrifices to defend a stand on the issue. Or ego involvement could refer to the degree to which the issue is tied to the self concept of the individual. You may be able to think of yet other definitions of ego involvement.

Similarly, the concept of participation could be viewed in a number of different ways. It might refer to total talk time. Or it could mean the number of contributions directly related to the issue rather than to socio-emotional needs of the participants. Or it might refer to defense of a position rather than making contributions intended primarily to be informative. It is apparent, then, that the researcher must define the key variables in a clear and consistent manner.

Consider a concept used in the study of romantic relationships, turning points. Turning points have been defined as "any event or occurrence that is associated with change in a relationship" (Baxter & Bullis, 1986). As you can see, it is important to clarify whether turning points refer only to externally visible events (such as a publicly announced engagement or moving to a new community) or to changes in internal states (realizing that one is in love) as well.

When the researcher is dealing with a variable that can have a variety of conceptual definitions, the researcher should identify the particular sense in which the term is being used in the project at hand. If the researcher fails to do this, the operational definition selected may have little to do with the rationale that motivated the study or the reader may be left puzzled about what a key variable really signifies.

PRECISION IN STATING THE RELATIONSHIP AMONG VARIABLES

In the physical sciences hypotheses frequently take the form of a formula that states precisely how much effect one variable has on another. In communication research, as in most social science research, such precision almost never exists.

The inability to specify exact relationships should not discourage attempts to be as precise as possible. For example, rather than simply hypothesizing that men and women will differ on some dimension, the researcher may be able to indicate the direction of the relationship—which gender is likely to display more of the type of behavior under consideration. Further, the researcher may even be able to offer a range of differences one might expect. For example, a hypothesis of this sort might assert that in a group discussion, women typically will express approval of comments made by others approximately twice as frequently as men. Such a claim does not predict that this relationship will hold in every case, but it is a more exact statement of the relationship than simply asserting that men and women differ in the extent to which they express approval of the comments of another in a group discussion.

Researchers should strive for precision in specifying both the direction and extent of relationships among variables.

Even the level of precision suggested above is not always attainable. One difficulty faced by communication researchers in trying to achieve precision is that we frequently lack a universal means of measuring a variable of interest. For example, although there have been many studies in which strength of fear appeal was manipulated, there is no single measure of strength of fear appeal; thus it remains difficult to synthesize the results of this body of work to produce more precise predictions. Nevertheless, communication researchers should strive for precision in specifying both the direction and extent of the relationships among variables.

SPECIFICATION OF THE SCOPE OF THE RELATIONSHIP

In addition to indicating the extent of the relationship among the variables, the researcher should attempt to describe the *scope of the relationship*, the conditions under which it is likely to exist. Consider this question: Is there a relationship between premarital conflict and marital satisfaction (Kelly, Huston, & Cate, 1985)? Clearly this is an important issue. With sustained research, it might be possible to specify the range of cases to which such a relationship applies. For instance, consider a more specific hypothesis: Couples who are in the top quartile (upper 25%) in premarital conflict are likely to fall in the bottom quartile (lower 25%) in marital satisfaction 2½ years after marriage. This hypothesis states a relatively precise relationship between the variables as well as indicating the types of couples to whom it applies.

Or suppose you were studying the impact of self disclosure by a stranger on an individual's liking of the stranger. It would be useful to specify the nature of the self disclosure (e.g., successes versus failures) and the typicality of the disclosure (unusual versus common events), among other features of the disclosure.

Of course the researcher does not always know the range of conditions under which the generalizations will hold true. And at times, the research question is directed toward discovering these conditions. But the researcher should identify as precisely as possible what is known about the conditions under which the hypothesis can be expected to obtain.

❏ Feasibility of Pursuing the Question

A second criterion for evaluating the worth of a research hypothesis or criterion is whether it is feasible to pursue. This issue obviously is of greater concern to the researcher than to the consumer.

The primary requirement for being able to produce an acceptable design is that the variables be conceived in ways that can be operationalized, that is, the variables can be translated to an observable form. For instance, consider the question: Does communication anxiety produce reticence to participate in social situations? This question is more difficult to translate to an observable form than one that defines the variables to be investigated more narrowly and concretely. Consider a narrower version of the same question: Do individuals who score high on a communication anxiety scale utter fewer statements that seem to initiate conversation with a stranger with whom they are spending 15 minutes awaiting an instructor than individuals who score low? We shall identify some of the factors that make it possible to move from a global question to one that is more concrete and amenable to study.

AVAILABILITY OF A DEPENDENT MEASURE

For each dependent variable, the researcher must have access to or be able to develop a measure that validly assesses the variable. In point of fact, whole areas of research frequently spring up simply because such a measuring instrument exists. For instance, when David Berlo (Berlo, Lemert, & Mertz, 1969-1970) and James McCroskey (1966) independently developed measures of credibility in the late 1960s, a body of literature on speaker credibility quickly emerged.

The ideal circumstance, of course, is for research to be guided by conceptual interests rather than by the availability of measuring instruments. The development of a valid measuring instrument is time consuming and does not always result in success. Thus the researcher may feel constrained by the availability of or capacity to develop an adequate measure of the dependent variable.

ETHICAL CONSTRAINTS ON USING MEASURES

Occasionally a situation exists in which it might be relatively easy to assess a variable, but the researcher is reluctant to do so for ethical reasons. Suppose a researcher were interested in the immediate impact of the death of a spouse on the survivor's desire to remarry. It is unlikely that any researcher would interrogate the spouse of a terminally ill person about his or her desire to remarry immediately before and after the death of a loved one.

In the field of communication, researchers sometimes face similar ethical constraints. For example, someone interested in relational communication might be reluctant to ask marital partners to describe their arguments in detail. Unless the researcher was able to offer assistance in resolving these grievances, focuses on these arguments could exacerbate their negative impact on the marriage.

Sometimes the need to protect the privacy of individuals makes it difficult or impossible to use available measuring instruments. For instance, intelligence and aptitude scores, which might be useful correlates in the study of the development of communication skills in children, typically are protected under privacy regulations, and rightfully so.

DIFFICULTIES MANIPULATING THE INDEPENDENT VARIABLE

Sometimes the researcher encounters difficulty in producing a realistic manipulation of the independent variable. For instance, suppose the researcher wants to study the impact on the decision made by a group of having the individual with the lowest status object to the decision preferred by the majority. The researcher would need to accurately identify the individual with the lowest initial status in each group. With careful pretesting, probably this could be done. Then, however, the researcher would need to induce the low-status participant to object to the will of the majority, and to do so as though it were the true feelings of this individual. Since many low-status individuals may not be accustomed to challenging the position of others, they might be reluctant to do so, and they might not be convincing, even if they were willing to try. Moreover, there would be logistic difficulties in knowing when the will of the majority had become solidified. It might be possible to overcome the difficulties just outlined, but it is obvious that manipulating the independent variable is not always easy.

DIFFICULTY GAINING ACCESS TO APPROPRIATE SUBJECTS

Frequently researchers encounter difficulty obtaining permission to approach the individuals who would be most appropriate as subjects. If a researcher were interested in employees' strategies for coping with the stress of knowing that their jobs were in jeopardy, one group of ideal subjects would be those working for an organization in serious financial difficulty. However, the management of such an organization might be hesitant to give permission to interview their employees for fear that focusing attention on the difficulties might heighten existing stress, make employees less effective, and thereby further jeopardize the future of the organization. Even if the researcher received permission to interview these employees, they might not talk freely, hoping that if some employees were retained, their jobs would be saved (Willihngang, 1988).

Gaining access to appropriate subjects can be problematic when research questions deal with sensitive issues, such as conflicts of an interpersonal or professional nature or feelings of inadequacy.

LOGISTIC DIFFICULTIES

Many of the problems encountered in doing research are purely logistic. For example, consider a field study conducted by Judee Burgoon and Lynn Aho (1982) in a department store. The authors were interested in the impact of the violation of interpersonal distance (a customer's standing too close or too far away from the sales clerk) on a number of nonverbal reactions of the sales clerk. The ideal method for data collection would have been to videotape the clerk during the episode and then to carefully code the nonverbal reactions later. However, because the researcher did not want the clerks to know that they were participating in a study, such a procedure was virtually impossible. Thus the researchers used observers who coded the clerks' nonverbal reactions as they occurred. When the researcher prefers to gather data under naturally occurring conditions, logistic arrangements can become difficult.

CONSTRAINTS IMPOSED BY LIMITED RESOURCES

One constraint every researcher faces is the upper bounds of the resources available. These most frequently take the form of limitations on time, money, equipment, and subjects. Most researchers would be delighted to use the sampling procedures offered by large survey organizations rather than relying so frequently on college students for subjects. But the many thousands of dollars required to hire the services of a survey organization often are not available. Therefore, researchers learn to optimize the resources available to them. And if careful in the way in which these resources are used, the research projects are still of high quality.

❑ Significance of the Question

By far the most difficult criterion to apply in judging the value of a research question or hypothesis is to evaluate the significance of the question itself. You would not expect perfect agreement among your classmates if asked to rate the significance of ten research questions. There are, however, guidelines that are useful in determining the significance of research questions.

IMPORTANCE OF THE PHENOMENON UNDER INVESTIGATION

Most of us would consider seeking a means of prevention for AIDS to be more important than seeking a means of prevention for dandruff. Clearly the impact of a phenomenon on our lives determines in large part the importance we attach to its study. For example, most of us again would rank research on the common cold as more important than research on dandruff, although we are not likely to die from either. A severe cold interferes with many activities we count as important: work, study, and sleep. Dandruff does not.

In general, then, phenomena tend to be considered more worthy of study if they have the potential to affect many facets of our lives that we consider important. Thus variables such as marital satisfaction, interpersonal attractiveness, and job satisfaction have received more attention than the number of dependent clauses an individual uses or the amount of energy expended in speaking at a certain decibel level.

Even with this general guideline of considering the impact of the phenomenon on lives, however, perfect agreement on the merits of phenomena for study cannot be achieved and even relatively close agreement will be difficult. For instance, we have not taken account of the number of people affected by the phenomena. Nor have we considered that individuals have different priorities. But these difficulties should not discourage either the researcher or the consumer of research from evaluating the significance of the phenomenon under investigation.

EXPLANATORY POWER

Some research questions deal with what we might call "surface level" variables and others with underlying relationships. For example, for several years researchers catalogued differences in men's and women's communicative behavior. Although this was useful, it had restricted explanatory power. Researchers were forced to rely on explanations that lay in the differences in the ways in which men and women were socialized. Although such explanations accounted for the differences in the behavior of many men and women, they did not account for nearly all. Consequently, some of the same researchers shifted their attention to an underlying variable, the desire for power. They felt that if they could identify individuals with a desire to exert power, they might more accurately predict differences in communication behavior along some dimensions than they could by simply classifying individuals as male or female. In general, then, variables that reflect the underlying phenomenon that produces the behavior have the potential to be of greater value than variables that simply classify directly observable phenomena.

Capacity to Synthesize Existing Research

In the field of communication, as in most fields, researchers sometimes become absorbed with a relatively narrow area of work and do not consciously link the work in this area to a broader framework. Occasionally a researcher comes along who offers a perspective that has potential to synthesize major existing areas of work and to suggest fruitful new avenues for

research. Such a perspective has enormous value, in part because it enables researchers in one area to use work from another area and in part because such a framework typically has
greater explanatory power than the initial perspectives. Thus
new approaches that provide a framework for integrating bits
and pieces of isolated work are extremely valuable.

A recent illustration of such a perspective is Barbara
O'Keefe's (1988) work on message logics. She identified three
basic logics, or views of what communication is designed to do,
and messages can be analyzed as emerging from one of the
three logics. The expressive logic is one in which individuals
view the function of communication as expressing whatever is
on their minds. The second is conventional, in which the function of communication is seen as saying whatever is appropriate in a given context. The third is rhetorical, in which the
function of communication is viewed as problem solving or
accommodating to the needs of all the participants in the situations. O'Keefe and her students have demonstrated that an
individual will tend to rely on one of these logics across a range
of situations.

The value of such a generalization is that it permits inte-
gration of a number of lines of research, for instance, work on
the use of persuasive message strategies and comforting message strategies. The content of the two sets of strategies was
different. Persuasive strategies referred to approaches such as
refuting counterarguments and offering advantages to the persuadee of complying with the request. Comforting strategies
included approaches such as diverting attention from the problem and expressing sympathy. By structuring each set of strategies into the more abstract categories identified by O'Keefe,
it becomes possible to formulate hypotheses about commonal-
ities across different domains of communication such as persuasion and comforting. Perspectives that offer an integrative
framework are rare. When they are formulated, they are worth
pursuing and refining.

In summary, then, it is important to evaluate the worth of
pursuing a given research question even though the criteria are

difficult to apply. This helps ensure the best use of the resources available.

❏ Study Questions

Divide into groups of four and evaluate the research questions below. Use the criteria discussed in the chapter you have just read to guide you evaluation: (a) clarity and precision of the question, (b) feasibility of pursuing the question, and (c) significance of the question.

1. Is there a difference between Americans and Japanese in their assertiveness in interpersonal conversations?
2. On what features of language do men and women differ in their usage?
3. Are romantic relationships in which there is now a low level of conflict prior to marriage likely to result in marriages that endure?
4. Do teenage males and females differ in their ability to construct comforting messages?
5. Are people who are high in self esteem also likely to be competent communicators?

3

Internal Validity of a Design

A second basic criterion for evaluating a study is the internal validity of the design. This is the single most important attribute of the study, because if there are weaknesses in the internal validity of the design, the study is of no value at all. *Internal validity* refers to the degree to which one can have faith in the results of the study, i.e., the degree to which the conclusions reached regarding the relationship among the variables studied accurately reflects their true relationship. Thus a study is internally valid when potentially contaminating variables have been appropriately dealt with. Otherwise we do not know whether variations observed in the dependent variable are due to manipulation of the independent variable or to some other contaminating variable. A well designed study that is internally valid rules out competing explanations for the results. If a study is not internally valid, nothing has been gained by conducting it. Note that internal validity refers only to the strength of the claims made within the constraints of the study, not to how far they should be generalized.

A well-designed study that is internally valid rules out competing explanations for the results.

A contaminating variable threatens the internal validity of a study by influencing the dependent variable differentially across experimental conditions. Put another way, a contaminating variable influences the dependent measure more in some conditions than in others. Suppose that we were studying the impact rate of speaking (independent variable) on comprehension (dependent variable). Comprehension might also be influenced by the difficulty of the message. Therefore we would not use a difficult message with one speaking rate and an easy message with the other. Otherwise we would not know whether any differences observed in comprehension were due to speaking rate (independent variable) or difficulty of the message (contaminating variable).

Or suppose, for instance, that I hypothesize that one teaching method is superior to another. I then have Professor Boring use on method and Professor Good another. At the end of the term I discover that Professor Good's students perform better than Professor Boring's, and I conclude that the method used by Professor Good is superior. But I may be totally in error. Perhaps Professor Boring is a poor instructor and his students would fare badly no matter what method he used. And Professor Good may be such a fine instructor that his students would perform well regardless of the method of instruction. In fact, Professor Good's students might have performed even better had he used the other method of instruction. In short, the study lacks internal validity. The conclusion that one instructional method is better than the other is not one we can put faith in, because we do not know whether the differences observed in students' performances are due to different teaching methods or to variations in the abilities of the instructors. In this case, skill of the instructors is a contaminating variable.

It is crucial to the internal validity of a study that it be designed to rule out competing explanations for the conclusions reached. Virtually every design choice the researcher must make has potential to influence the internal validity of the study. The most common problems researchers face with respect to internal validity are discussed in the next section. Others will become apparent in later chapters as we discuss specific choices to be made.

❑ Operational and Conceptual Definitions

One threat to the internal validity of a study is the possibility that the operational definition of an independent variable fails to adequately reflect its conceptual definition. In other words, the operational definition may fail to represent the essence of the concept it is designed to represent.

Consider the following hypothesis: As the number of hesitation phenomena in a message increases, the credibility of a speaker decreases. Now suppose that the number of hesitation phenomena is operationalized by inserting a pause between every nth word. For example, the researcher might use three different conditions of the independent variable: a pause every 15 words, every 10 words, and every 5 words. Clearly the researcher has manipulated the number of hesitations in a message and might well conclude that the greater the frequency of the hesitations, the lower the credibility of the speaker. But this conclusion might well be in error. In naturally occurring speech, hesitations do not occur at intervals of every nth word. They tend to occur at natural junctions of thought, frequently at the end of clauses or phrases. Had the hesitations been inserted at locations where they occur normally, the researcher might have found that a greater number of hesitations did not diminish the credibility of the speaker. As you can see, the internal validity of a study demands that the operational definition of independent variables truly reflect the essence of the variable they are designed to reflect.

It is relatively common to use a pre-test to determine whether an operational definition adequately reflects the concept represented in the independent variable. Consider a study which hypothesized that men would display more power in their speech (i.e., initiate conversation, speak longer, and gesture more) when speaking on topics more familiar to men than women, but that women would display more power when talking on topics more familiar to women (Dovidio, Brown, Heltman, Ellyson, & Keating, 1988). The independent variable, then, is gender-familiarity with topic (male versus female familiarity). To be sure that the particular topics used adequately reflected these categories, the researchers collected ratings of familiarity from men and women on a number of topics. In the main study the topics used were the ones that had showed the greatest differences between men and women in their familiarity with the topic.

❏ Dealing With Potentially Contaminating Variables

As we saw in Chapter 1, even if the researcher adequately operationalizes the independent variable, one can still draw an inaccurate conclusion if other potentially contaminating or confounding variables are not dealt with appropriately. In most studies, there are multiple factors that can potentially confound the results. In fact, we might control for a potentially contaminating variable without even realizing that was what we were doing. It would instinctively seem like the right thing to do. Suppose our hypothesis was that when a speaker from a minority ethnic group reflects clear understanding of a complicated technical issue, this speaker will be judged to have even higher credibility than a Caucasian who displays the same level of competence. (The assumption here is that when we negatively stereotype a group but are then confronted with direct evidence of competence of a member of that group, our evaluation of that individual becomes extremely positive.) The researcher could manipulate the ethnicity of the speaker by having a Caucasian speak to one audience and a member of an ethnic minority group speak to a different audience.

Quite likely if you were conducting the study, you would have the two speakers deliver the same message. If different messages were used, this would be a contaminating variable. Any differences found in the credibility ratings might then be due to the ethnicity of the speaker or to the content of the message, and there would be no way to know which was more influential. You might also instinctively try to ensure that the speakers themselves shared certain characteristics. For example, you might equate them in terms of sex, age, general attractiveness, and skill in speaking. Again, if you found differences in the credibility ratings of the two speakers but had failed to equate them on the dimensions just outlined, you would have difficulty arguing that the ethnicity distinction rather than another factor was responsible for the variation in the credibility ratings. There is always the danger, of course, that the researcher might not anticipate a factor that has potential to influence fluctuations in the dependent measure, in which case the internal validity of the study is undermined. As we shall see later, there are a variety of means available to the researcher for dealing with potentially confounding variables. If the study is to be internally valid, however, the researcher must anticipate variables that may influence dependent measure, and then deal with these variables appropriately.

❑ Assignment of Subjects to Experimental Conditions

In a true experiment subjects or participants are randomly assigned to experimental conditions. If subjects are not randomly assigned to the various conditions of an independent variable, then differences observed in the dependent measure may be due to differences in the groups of subjects themselves rather than to manipulation of the independent variable.

Suppose, for instance, that you wanted to study the impact of offering only corrective feedback (suggestions for improvement) in response to the performance of beginning public speaking students versus providing only positive feedback (praise for what was done well). Imagine that the researcher asked for volunteers at the beginning of the term for each of these conditions and concluded at the end of the term that students demonstrated a higher level of performance with corrective rather than with positive feedback. The difference in the performance of the two groups might in actuality have less to do with the feedback offered than with the kinds of students who selected each option. Students who opted for the corrective feedback condition may have already had excellent speaking skills and a high level of self confidence and been seeking ways of making minor improvements in their performances. Had the corrective feedback been used with less skilled and less self-confident students, it might have produced disastrous results. In sum, then, the researcher must avoid assigning subjects to experimental conditions in ways that result in variations in characteristics of the subjects across treatment conditions that may affect the dependent measure.

❏ The Relationship of the Measuring Procedure to the Dependent Variable

As you would expect, it is important that the dependent measure actually assess the essence of the dependent variable. Although no measuring procedure can capture all attributes of a variable, the dependent measure should reflect the most critical feature(s) of the dependent variable. A measuring instrument that assesses the attribute it is intended to measure is called a *valid instrument*. This should not be confused with the validity of the design itself, which is concerned with the relationship between the conclusions reached in the study and the procedures by which they were derived. Rather, the validity of an instrument refers to the relationship between what it actually assesses and what it is intended to assess.

Undoubtedly you have encountered charges that measuring instruments with which you are familiar are not valid. For instance, some educators claim that standard intelligence tests are not valid measures of the intellectual ability of minority groups because questions are culture bound. Others have argued that the standardized tests of ability frequently used for screening applicants to college and professional schools are not valid indicants of a student's ability to succeed. If these charges are accurate, then conclusions based on these measuring instruments are suspect.

If a dependent variable fails to assess what it was intended to, the conclusions drawn may be in error.

In the same way, if an experiment is conducted using an invalid measure of the dependent variable, the conclusions reached may be inaccurate. For example, suppose a project were designed to examine the impact of the importance of a group decision to an individual (independent variable) on the individual's amount of input to the decision (dependent variable). Imagine that the researcher manipulated the importance of the decision in such a way that it would have no real impact on some subjects, but for others it would significantly influence their final grade in a required course. Now assume that the measure of input was the number of times an individual initiated a comment during the discussion. Subjects who were unaffected by the decision might be more likely to serve a variety of functions during the discussion. For instance, they might attend to the socio-emotional and physical needs of others. Or they might serve procedural functions, such as summarizing, clarifying, and seeking information. By contrast, subjects with more at stake might restrict their comments to offering and evaluating substantive suggestions. At the end of the discussions, however, all comments, regardless of their content, would be counted as input. Thus the researcher might inaccurately conclude that subjects with nothing at stake had more input in the decision that subjects with much to gain or lose. In actuality, subjects whose grade hinged on the decision may have had much more input into the decision itself, but simply have initiated fewer total comments.

Clearly, then, if a dependent measure fails to assess what it was intended to, the conclusions drawn from the study may be in error. In short, the study then lacks internal validity.

❑ Context in Which Variables Are Embedded

As mentioned earlier, variables cannot be manipulated or assessed in a vacuum. They exist in a real context, and as you would expect, the nature of this context has the potential to influence the internal validity of the design. Some contexts will be more favorable than others for producing the kind of relationship projected in the hypothesis.

For example, imagine that the hypothesis is that speeches that cite six authoritative sources are more persuasive than those that cite fewer than six. Such a prediction might be likely to be true if the speeches were given by individuals who initially were not thought to be experts themselves. By contrast, if the speeches had been presented by individuals perceived by their audiences to be leading experts, the inclusion of evidence from others might have made no differences at all.

One way of dealing with this problem, that the hypothesis is true under one set of conditions but not under another, is to specify more precisely the conditions under which it is expected to obtain.

Note that the problem outlined above does not always lead to confirmation of a false hypothesis. In the illustration cited above, the context can lead to failure to support a hypothesis that would have been confirmed under a different set of circumstances.

On the other hand, there are times when a hypothesis is supported even under circumstances unfavorable to its confirmation. In these instances, the design is internally valid and, moreover, provides particularly strong evidence for the conclusion reached under adverse circumstances. For instance, in an early study conducted by Stafford Thomas (1969) on the comprehension of words from an audiotape, he hypothesized that comprehension is better when the delivery is varied than when it is monotonous. The hypothesis was confirmed. Since subjects were participating in a classroom test-like situation, they quite likely were attentive and motivated to do their best to comprehend the stimulus material. Had they been free to ignore the monotonous stimulus material, the difference between comprehension under varied and monotonous conditions might have been even more pronounced, thereby providing even stronger support for the hypothesis.

It is clear that regardless of whether the conditions in which the variables are embedded render it easier or more difficult to support an hypothesis, they have enormous potential to influence the results of a study.

❑ Study Questions

Divide into groups of four and discuss the following:

1. What is meant by the internal validity of a design? Why is it important? What is its relationship to the external validity of a design?
2. In what way can unclear definitions damage the internal validity of a design?
3. What is a potentially contaminating variable? What is its relationship to the internal validity of a study?
4. How can assignment of subjects to experimental conditions affect the internal validity of a study?
5. How does the context in which the variables are embedded influence the internal validity of a design?

4

External Validity of a Study

The final criterion for evaluating the worth of a study is its external validity. *External validity* refers to the generalizability of the results of a study. To the extent that the results of a study are generalizable to a wide range of situations, the study is said to be externally valid. As you can see, a study is neither externally valid or invalid, but possesses some degree of external validity.

It is not always possible to judge precisely the degree of external validity of a study at the time it is conducted. The true test of the external validity of a study is its replicability under widely divergent circumstances. Put another way, we have greatest faith in results that have been replicated by diverse methodologies.

Consider a specific line of research that was pursued by both experimental and descriptive studies, using different operational definitions each time. Stanley Schacter's (1974) work on obesity yielded the generalization that obese patients eat in response to external cues, whereas normal weight people eat in response to internal cues or to their physiological needs. Some of his work was descriptive observation of naturally occurring phenomena. He found that obese patients were more likely than their normal weight counterparts to abandon meal contracts in dormitories (the assumption that they were seeking better tasting food rather than meeting nutritional needs). Overweight pilots flying across time zones tended to eat a meal in the new location rather than at a natural interval following their previous meal. And in some instances, overweight individuals actually ate less than their normal weight counterparts as a response to internal cues. In particular, they were more likely to fast on religious holidays.

> The true test of the external validity of a study is its replicability under widely divergent circumstances.

Schacter's experimental work used a variety of manipulations of external cues. Altering perceptions of time by manipulating the face of a clock affected the consumption of overweight individuals, but not normal weight ones. When the food provided was unappealing, overweight people ate less than normal weight ones, whereas the opposite was true when the food provided was appealing. In an attempt to demonstrate the underlying process, Schacter inflated balloons in subjects' stomachs, and observed that normal weight subjects were more accurate than overweight ones in perceiving their internal state (empty or full).

In each of the studies just cited, it might be possible to identify potentially contaminating variables. But the fact that the results of the entire line of work supported the same conclusions while using different methodologies lends enormous force to the conclusion.

Similarly, within the field of communication, a number of generalizations exist that are believable because they have been replicated many times using different methodologies. For instance, we tend to believe, at least with respect to issues that are not highly ego involving, that an audience will display more immediate attitude change when receiving a message from a highly credible source rather than a less credible one. We tend to believe that on the whole, individuals are attracted to others who share similar backgrounds, values, and interests. We also tend to believe that as children get older they produce messages that suggest greater awareness and accommodation to the needs of others. Disciplines are built on propositions that have been demonstrated over and over again under diverse sets of circumstances.

Clearly, then, the most fruitful research typically does not occur as an isolated study, but rather as part of a systematic line of work. Specifically, a hypothesis is tested and refined under a variety of circumstances. But each individual study should maximize its potential to contribute to a generalization that holds across a wide range of circumstances. Thus the most useful studies not only maximize internal validity, but also provide the greatest potential for generalizing the results to a broad range of circumstances. We shall now discuss a number of the factors that were outlined earlier as relevant to the internal validity of the study. This time, however, we will consider how they can influence the external validity of the results.

❏ Operational Definition of the Independent Variable

An independent variable can be operationalized so that it reflects the essence of the variable in a variety of contexts. It can also be operationalized in a narrow, idiosyncratic way that would make generalization to other circumstances difficult.

Consider a hypothesis posed a number of years ago concerning romantic attraction. The researchers posited that individuals are romantically attracted to others when physiologically aroused and also perceiving cues that would make it plausible to attribute the arousal to romantic attraction. Physiological arousal (independent variable) was manipulated in one study by telling subjects that they would be receiving mild electrical shocks. Half the subjects were later told that they would not receive shocks, presumably reducing arousal, whereas the other half still anticipated being shocked. All the subjects, who were male, then encountered an attractive female (a confederate working for the experimenter) who behaved in a friendly and supportive manner. The men who still expected shocks displayed greater liking for the confederate (dependent variable) than did those who did not anticipate shocks.

One might challenge the study on a number of grounds. For example, liking a person does not necessarily imply being romantically attracted to that person. The subjects might also have liked a pleasant, supportive male, or dog, for that matter, but clearly not have been romantically attracted to either.

But the primary concern about the operationalization of the independent variable's impact on the external validity of the study centers on the physiological arousal induced by apprehension of impending shocks. Clearly most people would never experience such a situation in the normal course of their lives. For the results to be generalizable, we must assume that the internal state produced by being told one is to receive electrical shocks is identical to the internal state produced by more ordinary circumstances that produce physiological arousal in our daily lives, at least in terms of their impact on romantic attraction. This assumption seems tenuous at best. A preferable design would have been to manipulate physiological arousal by a procedure similar to ones that actually do produce this state in our daily lives. For instance, many of us feel some arousal when we know that the dentist is about to drill one of our teeth or when we are about to take a final examination that we have heard is very difficult. With some reflection, the researcher should be able to generate a manipulation that seems more likely to approximate real-life experiences that are typically of a reasonably broad range of circumstances.

❏ Dependent Measure

By the same line of reasoning, the researcher should select a dependent measure that captures the essence of the dependent variable, not some narrow or tangential aspect of the dependent variable. In the study cited above, for instance, the measure of romantic attraction was a scale designed to assess liking. Although liking would seem to be a component of romantic attraction, it would not seem to be its essence. We like lots of people, events, and objects, but would not consider ourselves romantically attracted to them. The researcher needed to select or develop an instrument that tapped the unique features of romantic attraction in order to generalize results of the study to that phenomenon.

❏ Subject Selection

Social scientific research frequently is criticized for using subjects who are not typical of the whole population. In fact, a frequent charge is that we know a great deal about college sophomores and not much about anybody else. Certainly it is true that much of the social scientific research, including communication research, is conducted with college students as subjects.

The crucial question, then, is to what extent this limits the generalizability of our results. For some kinds of hypotheses and questions, relying on one kind of subject presents real difficulties.

Certainly using only one type of subject will place severe limitations on our ability to derive generalizations from descriptive research that quantify scores or identify norms for a dependent variable. For instance, you would not want to generalize about how much pizza the average human consumes by studying the pizza consumption of the average American college sophomore. By the same token, you should not try to identify the exact level of performance on some communication task (e.g., use of politeness strategies when refusing a request) based solely on the performance of children enrolled in a church-affiliated school in a southern state. The children may have been reared in homes where more emphasis was placed on protective feelings than children raised in a different type of environment.

> *Some generalizations that we have assumed to be true are in actuality culture bound.*

In fact, we are discovering that some generalizations that we have assumed to be true are in actuality culture bound. As we expand our subject pool for Americans to include people of other nationalities, we are encountering the need to modify or revise some of our principles. For instance, for some time self disclosure was considered a relatively positive phenomenon that engendered a sense of intimacy. As we investigate the reactions of Asians, however, it becomes apparent that they respond less favorably to the disclosure of personal information than to Americans. Sugimoto (1990), for instance, found that the Japanese judge individuals who disclose a success and attribute it to their ability as less likable than Americans do. Similarly, Asians may prove more likely than Americans to avoid the use of linguistic forms that place obligations on others.

Other subject characteristics, such as gender or age, also restrict generalizations. There is a growing literature that suggests a variety of ways in which men and women differ in communicative style. Sillars, Weisberg, Burgraf, and Wilson (1987), for example, summarize some of the research relevant to marital communication that identifies differences in the communicative styles of men and women. And there are an enormous number of ways in which children's communication is not identical to that of adults.

In summary then, any generalization that attempts to quantify specific responses must be scrutinized carefully for possible bias resulting from selection of a particular type of subject. It is perfectly appropriate, of course, to modify the hypothesis itself to reflect the limitations imposed by subject selection. But the researcher must ensure in some manner that the conclusion reached reflect the particular type of subjects used.

By contrast, a different sort of hypothesis may suffer less from use of a restricted pool of subjects. In particular, true experiments may manipulate an independent variable in order to assess the *relative* impact of different conditions of the independent variable on the dependent measure. The key factor in this kind of research is that the researcher is not trying to determine absolute scores, but rather to determine the *relative differences* in scores produced by alternative conditions of the independent variable.

Consider a particular case. Suppose the researcher is interested in determining whether training children to use politeness strategies when refusing a request actually increases the use of these politeness strategies. In this project the researcher is interested in the difference between the scores of children who receive instruction and those who do not, rather than how high or low the actual scores are. Thus, if this researcher had used a group of children enrolled in a church-related school in the South, the results might not have been biased. It might not have mattered that both the children who received training and those who did not scored higher than another group of children might have as long as the *difference* between the children who received training and those who did not was the same as it would have been with another set of subjects. Of course, you can imagine circumstances in which even the difference in scores produced by manipulation of the independent variable might not be the same for two different sets of subjects. For example, the children in the southern parochial school could all have been initially so polite that instruction in politeness strategies had little impact. With another group of subjects, who were initially less polite, the training might have produced a substantial increment in scores. The researcher, therefore, must attempt to judge whether the difference in scores obtained across conditions is approximately the same degree of difference one might expect of a different type of subjects had been used.

For much communication research, however, reliance on the college sophomore does not seem particularly problematic. Think about the research on credibility that has fairly consistently shown that there is a greater initial attitude change when a message is authored by an individual with high rather than low credibility when the issue is not highly ego involving. It may well be that college students differ from other groups in which particular individuals they consider to be highly credible. But they may respond very much like any other group of people in their reactions to sources with high versus low credibility. In such an instance, the researcher must take care, of course, to ensure that, with the particular group of subjects used, the sources truly are perceived to have the level of credibility intended.

In summary, the results of a study using sophomore college students as subjects will have as much generalizability as the results using any other group as subjects if the *differences* produced by manipulation of the independent variable are comparable to the differences used using any other group, regardless of the absolute magnitude of the scores.

❏ Conditions in Which the Variables Are Embedded

Sally Jackson and Scott Jacobs (1983) have highlighted one of the most significant difficulties in generalizing the results of research in communication. They identified needless restrictions on the conditions in which the variables are embedded. Much of the communication research embeds the independent variable in a message. For instance, Canary and Spitzberg (1987) studied ratings of the appropriateness and effectiveness of three types of strategies for dealing with conflict that were embedded in message scripts. If a single basic message, or even several messages, are used throughout the study, we still know only how the variable operates in the context of that particular message or set of messages. They argue that it is both possible and desirable to embed the appropriate condition of any independent variable in a different message for each subject. By so doing, the researcher can then claim that the manipulation of the independent variable has a particular effect in a wide range of specific contexts.

Consider for a moment how our failure to use multiple messages in communication research can potentially bias the results. Even with a generalization as well documented as the one that messages produce more initial attitude change when coming from a highly credible source than from a less credible one, such bias is possible. Imagine that the particular messages used to test this hypothesis were exceptionally well reasoned and documented. If such a message had been used in the initial study, and only one message had been employed, the researcher might have found little difference in the attitude change generated by the high credibility source and the low credibility source because the context of the message was itself highly persuasive. In this way, use of a single message might have led us to abandon the credibility of the source as an influential factor in attitude change.

Similarly, much of our work on how group decisions are made is restricted to groups that meet solely for the purpose of the study. The participants know nothing about each other, the decision has no real consequences for them, and they probably will never see each other again. The dynamics of such a group may not bear a strong resemblance to real groups. Participants in real groups bring prior attitudes toward each other, may have a lot to risk in the decision, and are likely to continue to interact with each other long after the particular decision is reached. It may be difficult, therefore, to generalize about the decision-making process from these artificially constructed groups to real groups.

To summarize, conclusions have greater external validity if they are derived from observation of a variety of specific contexts and from ones that are typical of real communication situations and are widely varied. Needless to say, this increases the work of the researcher, but it yields enormous dividends in the generalizability of the results. At a minimum, the researcher should specify as precisely as possible the range of circumstances to which the results can be generalized.

❑ Study Questions

Divide into groups of four and discuss the following:

1. What is meant by the external validity of a design and why is it important?
2. What are some of the major factors that influence the external validity of a design?
3. For each of the following questions, suggest a design that you feel enhances the external validity of the design. Justify your choice.
   a. Employees who are given a lot of feedback by supervisors are more satisfied than those who receive minimal feedback.
   b. When reprimanding another individual for failing to fulfill an obligation, the person receiving the reprimand will be less resentful if he or she is first given the opportunity to explain why the failure occurred than if not given such an opportunity.
   c. Following initial interaction with a stranger, individuals tend to underestimate how favorable an impression the other person formed of them.

5

Operationalizing the Independent Variable

The researcher faces a series of major decisions related to instantiating or operationalizing each independent variable. The *instantiation* or *operational definition* of a variable refers to a set of procedures for producing specified conditions of the variable or procedures for assessing particular states of the variable. In other words, an operational definition or instantiation of a variable provides an observable representation of an abstract variable. (Recall that there is no theoretical limit on the number of independent variables.) The first, and probably most crucial, decision is whether to manipulate the variable (experimental research) or to identify existing conditions of the variable (descriptive research). The researcher then must determine the number of levels or conditions of the variable to be used, whether to include subsidiary variables, and how to deal with potentially contaminating variables. This last matter, the means of coping with variables that can confound the results, is a crucial decision. Each of these decisions is discussed below.

❑ Manipulation Versus Identification of Existing Conditions

As discussed earlier, the researcher may or may not be faced with the decision of whether to manipulate conditions of a variable. Some variables cannot be manipulated directly (e.g., the age of the communicator). With such variables, the only manipulation possible would be *perceptions* of that variable. For instance, written communications might be used and *attributed* to individuals of varying ages. Or actual speakers might be used and the perception of age could be manipulated through use of makeup and acting techniques.

For many variables, however, the researcher faces a true choice of whether to manipulate or select existing conditions of a variable. Consider, for instance, the hypothesis that individuals tend to like strangers who disclose a minor failure during an initial casual conversation better than those who describe a minor success. The researcher might manipulate the disclosure in a setting where students from different speech communication classes were waiting to participate in a study. Confederates working with the researcher could be trained to initiate conversation with the individual sitting next to them and, during the conversation mention that they were receiving either moderately high or moderately low grades in their communication course. On the other hand, in the same circumstance, but without use of confederates, the researcher could record conversations of waiting students and have the recordings coded to identify conversations in which either moderately positive or moderately negative information was revealed.

How does the researcher decide which approach to take? Practical considerations may become a factor. The researcher might elect to use naturally occurring disclosures, but after

recording several hundred conversations, decide that disclosures occur too infrequently to be useful. Moreover, as we
discussed earlier, each approach has a distinct
advantage. Manipulation of a variable helps
ensure that only the variable of interest (disclosure of success or failure) is altered. In the case
which the researcher observed the naturally
occurring disclosures, there may have been
other differences as well. For example, people
who made disclosures may have in general
been more outgoing and friendly than people
who made no disclosures and thereby have
generated a favorable impression of themselves regardless of the nature of their disclosure. Thus a primary feature of the manipulation is that it
isolates the variable from the other factors with which it is
normally associated. Whether this is desirable depends on the
rationale underlying the project. If the researcher is interested
in how the variable operates in its normal context, then the
descriptive approach of identifying the existing conditions of
the variable is preferable. If the researcher wants to know how
the variable operates in isolation, then manipulation is more
desirable.

A primary feature of manipulation is that it isolates the variable from other factors.

You can imagine reasons why the researcher might be interested in the variable in isolation. For example, the researcher
might want to know whether disclosure or simply general
willingness to talk with a stranger is more responsible for the
impression formed. This might be of importance if you wished
to *alter* behavior. Suppose you were working with a group of
individuals who have difficulty making friends. You could
advise them to avoid discussing their successes in initial conversations with others if you discovered that doing so yields
less liking in initial encounters.

By contrast, identifying existing conditions of the variable
tends to be a better way of observing how that variable operates in its normal context. Moreover, identifying existing conditions also typically gives greater assurance that a realistic

instantiation of the variable is being used. Manipulation may fail to accurately reflect the way disclosure occurs naturally, or it may fail to adequately represent the wide range of forms that disclosure may take. Thus the researcher must weigh the relative advantages of manipulating versus identifying existing conditions of a variable to determine which approach better serves the rationale for pursuing the question. This choice determines, of course, whether the researcher is conducting an experiment (in which the variable is manipulated) or a descriptive study (in which existing conditions of the variable are identified).

❑ Manipulation Checks or Assessing Existing Conditions of the Variable

Frequently manipulation of an independent variable is accompanied by a manipulation check. A *manipulation check* represents an attempt to assess whether the manipulation of the independent variable has produced the conditions of the independent variable that were intended. Consider again the question of whether revealing a minor success or a minor failure leads to more liking by a stranger. The researcher needs to be certain that what he or she thinks of as a success or a failure is viewed the same way by the participants in the study. Thus the researcher would need to identify events that presumably fall into each of these categories and actually assess whether they are viewed that way by individuals similar to those who will serve as subjects in the main study. Obtaining identification of these events as either successes or failures by individuals similar to the subjects in the main study is a manipulation check because it represents an attempt to verify that the independent variable has been successfully manipulated.

The time when the manipulation check is administered is of some importance. Typically the researcher will administer a manipulation check prior to collection of the primary data using subjects similar to those to be used in the main study. In this way the researcher avoids investing effort in the main study until the independent variable has been manipulated successfully. Conducting a manipulation check prior to the main study is one form of a pre-test.

The researcher may administer the manipulation check a second time, during the main study itself. When this is done, the researcher typically introduces the primary dependent measures before administering the manipulation check. This is done to avoid alerting the subjects to the nature of the manipulation. Suppose the subjects were asked to indicate whether the disclosure by the stranger should be considered a success or a failure *before* they were asked how much they liked the stranger. They would realize that the researcher expected to find a link between the kind of disclosure and their liking. This realization might bias their responses. For instance, subjects might feel obligated to react more strongly to the disclosure than they normally would. Consequently, a better procedure would be to measure liking first and then to determine whether the disclosure had been considered a success or a failure.

What we have been calling a manipulation check is a procedure that is commonly used in descriptive research. That is, individuals' responses are used to assess what we referred to earlier as a predictor variable. Suppose, for instance, that the researcher was pursuing the same question posed above, but this time was using a descriptive rather than an experimental study. This time the disclosure of successes or failures would not be manipulated. But the researcher might use a procedure similar to the manipulation check to determine whether in naturally occurring conversations with a stranger, the stranger had revealed any successes or failures.

Or the researcher might not wait for the conversations to occur in a natural environment. The researcher might put two strangers together and ask them to talk for fifteen minutes (not manipulating the disclosures of either). Following the conversation, the researcher could ask the individuals to indicate whether the other interactant had revealed any successes or failures. Since no manipulation of an independent variable took place, this would be a descriptive rather than an experimental study despite the fact that the researcher contrived the circumstance in which to observe behavior. Just as with the manipulation check, it would be preferable to assess liking before asking the participants to identify the type of self disclosure to avoid implying that a link between the two variables ought to exist.

❑ Taking Account of Initial Differences in Subjects' Reactions

Frequently the independent variable is an internal state of a person, rather than an external condition. The researcher must decide whether to use the same external manipulation for all subjects, or to alter the manipulation to accommodate to individual differences in subjects. For example, imagine that the research hypothesis is that the individuals will use less cooperative decision-making processes when the outcome of the decision has great importance to the individual than when it is of little significance. The independent variable, importance of the outcome, must be manipulated. Importance of outcome is an internal state (perception by the subjects) rather than an external variable such as length of time permitted for discussion. Suppose, moreover, that the researcher plans to use students as subjects and, in order to achieve greatest external generalizability, is going to use students of all ages (first graders through graduate students). A manipulation that might vary the importance of the outcomes for some participants might not for others. For example, the group task might be to determine within five minutes which three of six people on a doomed ship deserved space on the last life raft. College students might be told that they would have their grade for that segment of the course raised by one letter if the group reached consensus within five minutes. College students might find this outcome (a grade increment) highly important, but first graders might not. First graders, on the other hand, might find the offer of candy for reaching consensus quickly to be a more important outcome than college students would.

In cases where the variable is an internal state (in this instance, the importance attached to the reward), the researcher must decide whether the actual *manipulation* should be the same for all subjects or the *internal state* should be more comparable for all subjects. In the instance of importance of outcome, maintaining comparability of the internal state requires pretesting alternative manipulations to determine which ones yielded similar internal states.

❑ Determining the Number of Levels of the Independent Variable

Once the researcher has completed the decisions regarding the manipulation of each independent variable, a decision must be reached concerning the number of conditions or levels of each independent variable. You cannot, of course, manipulate a variable without at least two conditions to compare with each other. But there is no theoretical limit on how many additional levels are possible. Suppose, once again, that the researcher is studying the impact on liking of a stranger with disclosure of a success or failure. The comparison might be made between a minor success and a minor failure. Or a third condition, mixed (both a success and a failure) could be added. Or five levels could be studied: Major success, minor success, mixed, minor failure, and major failure. You could, of course, continue to expand the number of levels or conditions theoretically to as many as represented true distinctions in the variable.

Consequently, the researcher needs criteria for determining the optimal number of conditions of each independent variable. The first consideration typically is a practical one, the availability of subjects. Each level or condition must contain enough subjects to give the researcher sufficient statistical power (a concept discussed later), so the researcher is seldom free to use an unlimited number of conditions of the independent variable.

But how few conditions can be used to adequately test the hypothesis, and which particular conditions should be used? These are important decisions facing the researcher.

The answer to the first question, how many levels or conditions should be used, depends in large part on the anticipated relationship between the independent and dependent variable. If a monotonic (straight line relationship) is expected, fewer conditions of the independent variable are necessary than if a curvilinear relationship is expected. A *straight line relationship* is one in which an increase in one variable corresponds consistently to either a specifiable increase or decrease in the other variable. For example, if there are no counteracting factors, the more calories a person consumes, the more weight that person gains.

By contrast, in a *curvilinear relationship* an increase in one variable corresponds to an increase in another variable for some values of the first variable, but to a decrease for other values. For instance, the number of hours an individual spends awake increases with age from birth to some point in middle age. Beyond that point in a person's life, further increase in age corresponds to fewer, not more, waking hours.

As you can see in this last example, if the researcher used only two conditions of the variable age, perhaps 5 years of age versus 65 years, the conclusion reached might well be that age is not related to the number of waking hours. If five different levels of age were used, however (perhaps 5, 15, 30, 50, and 75 years of age), the true curvilinear relationship would become more evident.

In our illustration of the impact of disclosures on liking, it is possible that the relationship might be curvilinear, once again making it desirable to use a number of conditions. For instance, if the individual revealed a major failure, a stranger might consider the individual a loser. If the individual revealed a major success, it might seem to be bragging. It is possible, therefore, that greatest liking would occur in the more moderate conditions of revealing a minor success or a minor failure or both.

The point is that the researcher's understanding of the variables under investigation should yield insight into the question of the possibility of a curvilinear relationship. If such a possibility exists, at least three levels of the independent variable should be used. Certainly, whether the relationship is curvilinear or straight line, the precision with which the relationship can be specified between any two variables is greater when a larger number of levels of the independent variable is used.

❑ Extremity of Conditions

When only two or three conditions of the independent variable are to be manipulated, the choice of which particular conditions or levels to use is a crucial decision. Suppose once again that the researcher is investigating the impact on the impression formed by a stranger of disclosure of personal successes or failures. The researcher must decide how extreme the information disclosed should be. For instance, the negative information might be that the individual had made a low grade on an examination, had been fired from a job for the second time that year, or had just been convicted on a child abuse charge. You can easily imagine that a stranger would react quite differently to each of these revelations. They may differ in effect, in part, because the first implies incompetence, the last suggest immorality, and the other could reflect either incompetence or immorality. In this case, the researcher might want to define independent variable more narrowly. That is, the variable could be defined as the disclosure of information revealing one to be moral or immoral. But even with a more precise definition of the independent variable, the researcher would still be confronted with the decision of how extreme to make the conditions of the independent variable.

How does the researcher decide how extreme the conditions of the variable should be? One more criterion for making this choice is to select the conditions that reflect typical levels of the variable in normal life. It is easier to imagine a stranger mentioning having received a low grade than having been convicted on a child abuse charge. In other words, the researcher should select a level of the variable that might actually occur without manipulation.

Moreover, in a case such as the one described, the researcher should explicitly identify the limitations of the study, for it is possible that a curvilinear relationship may exist between the level of negativity of the disclosure and the negativity of the impression formed. For instance, if a stranger mentions having received a low grade, this may generate sympathy and produce a reasonably positive impression. But if a stranger mentions having been convicted on a child abuse charge, this may generate a sense of revulsion and result in a negative impression. Hence if the researcher is able to use only one condition and selects a typical one, the report of the study might acknowledge the possibility of a different outcome with a more extreme manipulation.

One difficulty in reporting with precision the level of the manipulation used is that, for the most part, we lack standardized measures for assessing the level of a variable. Unlike physical scientists who have standardized variables for much of what they do, communication researchers lack universal measures of variables such as the negativity of a self disclosure. Development of such measures would make it possible to specify more precisely the relationship among the variables we study.

❑ Selection of Additional Variables

Thus far we have concentrated on issues related to manipulation of a single variable of interest to the researcher. Another major decision faced by the researcher is whether to include additional independent variables. These variables may not have been of sufficient concern to motivate the study initially, but are of some interest. There are two reasons that the researcher might want to do so.

Perhaps the most common reason for including an additional variable is the researcher's belief that it interacts with a primary variable. An *interaction between independent variables* means that their combined impact could not be detected by studying the impact of each in insolation from the other. Put another way, the influence of one independent variable on the dependent is contingent upon the particular condition of the other independent variable.

Consider an illustration. The researcher is interested in the influence of two variables on attitude change: speaker credibility and inclusion of evidence. If the researcher studies each of these variables in isolation from the other, the studies may yield the conclusion that sources with high credibility produce more attitude change than sources with low credibility and that inclusion of five pieces of evidence produces more attitude change than inclusion of no evidence. From these two generalizations, readers might infer, then, that the greatest attitude change related to these variables would occur when a highly credible source includes five pieces of evidence. But this may not be true. If credibility of the source and inclusion of evidence interact in their impact on attitude change, they must be studied in conjunction with each other, not in isolation.

Including variables both in the same design might yield the following results. In general, sources with highly credibility generate more attitude change than sources with low credibility, inclusion of five pieces of evidence produces more attitude change than use of no evidence. But for a highly credible source, the amount of attitude change generated is the same with five pieces of evidence and with no evidence at all, because this source is very believable to begin with. In this case, credibility and inclusion of evidence are said to interact. If the researcher had studied the two variables in separate studies rather than in conjunction with each other, the conclusion that the greatest attitude change occurs when a highly credible source uses five pieces of evidence might have been incorrectly drawn. Thus one common reason for including more than one independent variable in a study is to determine whether it interacts with a primary variable.

One reason for including more than one independent variable is to determine whether it interacts with a primary variable.

Recall the study cited earlier (Dovidio, Brown, Heltman, Ellyson & Keating, 1988) in which it was hypothesized that men would display more power in communicating about topics highly familiar to males but that women would display more power when communicating about topics more familiar to females. Here the dependent variable is displaying of power and the variables treated as independent variables are gender of the communicator (which obviously is categorized rather than manipulated) and familiarity of the topic to each gender. Rather than predicting that in general men display more power than women (or the contrary), the hypothesis involves an *interaction* of the variables of gender of communicator and topic familiarity. The prediction indicates that the power displayed by either men or women *is contingent upon the specific condition of another variable*, the familiarity of the topic to that gender. As you can see, it is frequently possible to generate more precise predictions by including additional independent variables.

The second reason for including additional variables is almost the converse of the first. The researcher believes that two variables do *not* interact, and wishes to verify this assumption because others hold the view that the variables do, in fact, interact. For instance, suppose researchers were interested in studying the impact of instruction on the use of politeness strategies on children's request refusals. Imagine that the researcher reported that such instruction increased the usage of politeness strategies. Some readers might assume that more

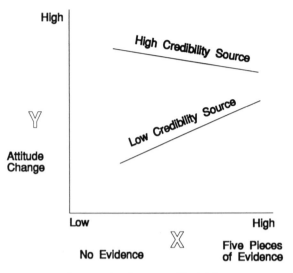

Interaction between Variables

improvement occurred among girls than boys, since girls are thought by some to be more interested in protecting feelings. Thus the readers would assume that an interaction exists between the variables of instruction and gender of the children. The researcher could include both instruction and gender as independent variables in the same study. If an interaction was found, the reader's suspicion that girls would profit more from instruction than boys might then be demonstrated. But if the researcher was correct in thinking that both sexes would profit approximately equally from the training, then no interaction effect would emerge. Inclusion of both independent variables makes it possible to resolve this question in the initial study.

❏ Dealing With Potentially Contaminating Variables

As you may recall from our discussion of the internal validity of a study, one of the most crucial decisions the researcher faces is how to deal with potentially contaminating variables. If a factor other than the independent variables influence variations in the dependent variable, then internal validity of the study (i.e., the believability of the results) is severely jeopardized. Consider an illustration. Imagine that the researcher is interested in the impact of the presence or absence of compliments on the degree of liking an individual reports following initial interaction with a stranger. You can immediately think of a host of variables other than compliments that might affect the degree of liking. Certainly one such variable is the general friendliness of the stranger. The researcher has four basic options for dealing with such a variable: holding it constant, allowing it to fluctuate randomly, systematically varying it as an additional independent variable, or allowing it to vary randomly but holding its effects constant statistically. We will consider the advantages and limitations of each of these alternatives.

HOLD THE POTENTIALLY
CONTAMINATING VARIABLE CONSTANT

Sometimes it is possible to hold a potentially contaminating variable constant across all conditions of the independent variable. This approach could be used in the illustration cited above. The same confederate could be used in both the condition in which the stranger issued compliments and the condition without compliments. The interactions could be recorded and coded to ascertain that the confederate's general level of friendliness was roughly equivalent across the two conditions.

Had this precaution not been taken, it would have been difficult to have faith in the results. Suppose that different confederates had been used in the compliment and no-compliment conditions and differences had been found in the level of liking in the two conditions. We would not know whether this difference was due to compliments or to some feature, such as friendliness, of the confederates themselves.

Holding a potentially contaminating variable constant has the advantage of guaranteeing that the variable does not bias the results. On the other hand, it restricts the external generalizability of the study, because it is possible to conclude only that when a stranger displays the general level of friendliness reflected by this particular confederate, that the impact of compliments is of the sort observed in this study.

RANDOMIZING THE EFFECT OF THE POTENTIALLY CONTAMINATING VARIABLE

A second approach to dealing with a potentially confounding variable is to allow it to function vary randomly. This approach assumes that, while the variable will fluctuate from case to case that is observed, *on the average* the impact of this variable will be about the same for each condition of the independent variable.

In the illustration cited above, the randomization approach might be implemented by using a different confederate for each interaction. If there were 50 subjects in the compliment condition and 50 subjects in the no-compliment condition, then each of the 100 subjects would be paired with 100 different confederates. Although the confederates almost certainly would differ in the level of friendliness they exuded, the average level of friendliness should be roughly equivalent in the compliment and no-compliment conditions.

The major advantage to this approach is that it affords greater external generalizability than the approach of holding the variable constant, because whatever conclusion is reached at the end of the study should hold true across the range of friendliness exhibited by all the confederates used in the study.

There are two limitations, however. The first is purely practical. Using 100 confederates is more difficult than using one. Not only must they be available, but they must be trained to offer compliments in the same manner. The second limitation is the possibility that the impact of the potentially contaminating variable will not turn out to be the same across all conditions of the independent variable. For example, by pure chance, the confederates might happen to be friendlier in one condition than the other. This possibility could be monitored, however, if the interactions were recorded and later coded for level of friendliness displayed. If a discrepancy in the average level of friendliness across conditions is found, the researcher might need to collect additional data.

INCLUDE THE POTENTIALLY CONTAMINATING VARIABLE AS AN ADDITIONAL INDEPENDENT VARIABLE

A third option for dealing with a potentially contaminating variable is to include it in the design as an additional independent variable. For instance, the general level of friendliness of the stranger could be manipulated by training confederates to display varying levels of friendliness to different subjects.

Such an approach has the primary advantage of permitting more precise conclusions to be drawn about the effect of the potentially contaminating variable. For example, use of compliments might increase the liking of an individual who otherwise displays little friendliness, but have little impact on the liking of individuals who are moderately or very friendly. Thus in cases where the potentially confounding variable interacts with the primary independent variable, including it as an independent variable is the preferred option. This approach does, of course, increase the number of subjects needed and requires a means of adequately manipulating the variable. Its limitations, as you can see, are practical, not conceptual.

HOLD THE IMPACT OF THE POTENTIALLY CONTAMINATING VARIABLE CONSTANT STATISTICALLY

The final option for dealing with a potentially confounding variable is to allow it to vary randomly, but to hold its impact constant statistically. This is possible only when the researcher can measure its fluctuation as it varies randomly.

This process works very much like a handicap works for golfers. Using a handicap, you determine which golfer had the better score for that round *if they had begun with the same level of ability*. In the same way, the impact of the conditions of the independent variable on the dependent variable are assessed as though the effect of the potentially contaminating variable had been held constant for all conditions.

This procedure begins much like randomizing a potentially contaminating variable does. For instance, in the illustration discussed above, the researcher might again use a different confederate for each interaction, perhaps 50 confederates for the compliment condition and another 50 confederates for the no-compliment conditions. This time, however, the researcher would have coders assess the general friendliness level of each confederate. These measurements then could be used to adjust each confederate's score, much as a golf handicap is used, so that the comparison between the use of compliments and no compliments would not be affected by any fluctuations in the friendliness level of the confederates.

This procedure of holding a potentially contaminating variable constant statistically serves the external validity of the study exceptionally well. The researcher is able to investigate the impact of the independent variable under a wide range of conditions of the potentially contaminating variable (in this case, general level of friendliness) without biasing the results. In fact, this approach is preferable to simply permitting the variable to operate randomly, because the researcher is *certain* that the impact of this variable is constant across all experimental conditions rather than assuming that the effect of the potentially confounding variable is roughly equivalent across conditions. It is more difficult to use, however, because it can be employed only when the researcher can measure the potentially confounding variable for every case used.

If the researcher can measure the potentially contaminating variables, the technique of holding constant the impact of potentially contaminating variables statistically is particularly useful in descriptive studies. Assume, for instance, that the researcher had videotapes of conversations that occurred among strangers, perhaps in a waiting room, and was able to obtain measures of liking from the participants shortly after the conversations. Then assume that the videotapes (with all compliments edited out) were evaluated by a panel of judges who rated the general level of friendliness displayed by each participant. The researcher could then assess the relationship between compliments and liking while statistically holding constant the impact of the general level of friendliness.

Permitting a variable to randomize its effects sometimes best maximizes external generalizability while minimizing practical limitations.

To review the four methods of dealing with confounding variables, we might conclude the following. Although it is frequently necessary for practical reasons, holding a potentially contaminating variable constant is the least desirable alternative from the standpoint of enhancing the external generalizability of the results. Both including the confounding variable as an additional independent variable and holding it constant statistically serve to extend the generalizability of the results, but involve practical limitations. Permitting a variable to randomize its effect across conditions sometimes offers the best compromise between serving the interests of external generalizability and minimizing practical limitations. In a given design the choice usually rests on the ability of the researcher to deal with practical problems involved in that particular case.

From the standpoint of the consumer, the most important factor is whether the researcher actually has dealt with potentially contaminating variables. When reading a research report, consider whether factors beyond the independent variable might account for variations in the dependent variable and whether the researcher has adequately dealt with this possibility.

❏ Study Questions

Divide into groups of four and consider the following hypothesis: In a discussion of views that differ from their own, participants who have much at stake in an issue will be more critical than participants who have little at stake. Answer the following questions.

1. Is it possible to study this question either by finding existing conditions of the independent variable or by manipulating the variable? If so, describe how this could be done in each case.
2. If you manipulated the independent variable, what kind of manipulation check could you use?
3. If you manipulated the independent variable, how many levels of the variable would you use? Why?
4. How extreme would you make the conditions of the independent variable? Why?
5. Are there additional independent variables that should be included in the design? If so, what are they?
6. With respect to the manipulation of the independent variable that you used, what are the potentially contaminating variables? How could you deal with them? Be as specific as possible.

6

Treatment of Subjects

Another set of decisions faced by the researcher concerns the individuals who will serve as subjects or participants for the project. The researcher must determine a method for initial selection of subjects in an experiment and a method for allocating them to experimental conditions. In addition, the researcher must make decisions that have potential to influence the subjects' orientation to the study and whether they are treated humanely.

❑ Subject Selection

First the researcher must decide if the results of the study should be confined to the individuals who participated in the study or generalized to a broader group. At times the researcher may have no interest in a larger population. For example, a

69

teacher may try a new instructional practice. The instructor uses the new practice with one class and the old method with another class and observes the outcome in a systematic fashion at the end of the term. If the instructor never plans to use the new practice again, it is not important to generalize beyond these two classes. But if the instructor wishes to be able to conclude that one method is *generally* preferable to the other, and thus ought to be used with other groups, then more care must be taken in determining what people will serve as subjects to compare the two teaching methods. In other words, if the instructor really hopes to generalize the results to a broader population, care must be taken that the groups used in the study adequately reflect a broader population.

A *population* is a group of individuals (or other type of experimental units) represented by the sample used in the study and to whom the results are to be generalized. A *sample* is the particular group of individuals (or other experimental units) selected from the population to participate in the study.

Ideally, if the researcher wishes the results to be generalized to a broader population, the first step of subject selection is to specify the characteristics of the population (maybe age, sex, or any other attribute thought to be relevant to the variables under investigation). The second step is to select a procedure for subject selection that will generate a sample representative of the population.

Researchers with ample resources typically follow both steps. Other researchers, however, constrained by lack of adequate resources, do not always engage in these procedures. Rather, they frequently rely on individuals who are available to serve as subjects, realizing that this procedure is less than ideal.

Since much communication research has been conducted in the latter fashion, relying on subjects who are accessible, we will review only the two most common procedures for selecting a representative sample and then consider the consequences of failing to use a representative sample.

RANDOM SAMPLING

With *random sampling,* every member of a population has an equal chance of being selected for the sample. This procedure presumes the ability to enumerate all members of the population and to employ a method that gives each individual equal opportunity for selection.

You can see immediately that enumerating all members of a population is a difficult, and sometimes impossible, undertaking. For instance, if the population was defined as all Americans over the age of 21, the particular members of this population are changing constantly. The second problem, of course, is ensuring that all members of the population have equal probability of being chosen. You can easily imagine the practical difficulties involved in actually gaining access to and cooperation from all members of a population. (Certainly the influx of illegal immigrants and the increase in the number of homeless individuals would exacerbate problems when the population is defined to encompass a broad sector of the American public.)

PROPORTIONAL STRATIFIED SAMPLING

Another procedure frequently used by marketing and other researchers is designed to produce a microcosm of a broad population with a relatively small sample. *Proportional stratified sampling* involves identifying a specific set of characteristics of the population considered relevant to the variable to be observed, and representing these characteristics in the sample in proportion to their incidence in the population. For example, if the behavior to be observed is whether or not an individual plans to vote, the characteristics of the population thought to be relevant might include age and percentage of times the individual has voted in the past. The population would then be stratified on these two characteristics to determine what percentage of the population possesses each particular combination of the two variables. Individuals who fit each particular combination of the characteristics would be chosen for the sample in proportion to their occurrence in the population. For example, if the researcher had decided to use a sample of 200 individuals, and 9% of the population was comprised of individuals age 30 and under who had voted in past elections less than 50% of the time, then 18 people would be selected randomly from that category of individuals.

Relying on subjects who are simply available rather than representative of a broader population may bias results.

The advantage of this procedure is that it produces a microcosm of the population using few subjects. The limitations, however, are both practical and conceptual. The researcher may have difficulty locating the appropriate number of subjects for each group. More seriously, the results may be biased if the characteristics on which the population is stratified are not, in reality, the ones that most strongly influence the variables to be observed. These characteristics should have been selected on the basis of prior research that documented their influence on the variable under investigation. The particular event being studied, however, might differ in some important way from those preceding it. For example, typically a smaller percentage of people under the age of 30 than people over 30 vote. But some issue in the selection being studied (perhaps regarding tax laws or sending troops to fight on foreign soil) might motivate a larger-than-normal proportion of young people to vote. If for any reason the circumstance being studied deviates substantially from the circumstance on which relevant characteristics of the population were chosen, the results may not accurately reflect the behavior of the population at large.

IMPACT OF BIAS IN THE SAMPLE

The researcher may not have the resources available to use true random sampling, proportional stratified sampling, or any other method that presumably would ensure that the sample adequately reflects relevant characteristics of the population. If forced to rely on use of subjects who are accessible rather than selected to be representative of a broader population, a key concern is the extent to which this can bias the results. You may recall that nonsystematic selection of subjects can influence the external validity of the results. Typically a nonrepresentative sample does not hinder the possibility of making statements about the *relative* impact of one experimental condition compared with another if subjects are randomly assigned to experimental conditions. It may, however, restrict the kinds of statements one can make about absolute scores on the dependent measure. In other words, if the researcher compared two methods of instruction using subjects who simply happened to be available, it would be possible to conclude that one method produced better results than another with these subjects, but it would be risky to predict the actual average scores that each method would be likely to yield.

❑ Assignment of Subjects to Conditions

The internal validity of a study depends in part on the procedure used to assign subjects to experimental conditions. The two major decisions that confront the researchers are whether to assign subjects to more than one experimental condition and what method to use to determine the particular condition(s) for each subject.

REPEATED MEASURES VERSUS INDEPENDENT GROUPS

If each subject is exposed to only one experimental condition, the design is called an *independent groups design*. If each subject is exposed to more than one experimental condition, the design is said to involve *repeated measures*, meaning that more than one measure of a single dependent variable is taken for each subject.

One advantage to using repeated measures is that fewer total subjects are required. Suppose that the researcher is investigating the impact of similarity on attraction. Subjects might be asked to rate potential roommates on their attractiveness as a roommate based on a written profile of the other person. Using this technique, each subject might be able to respond to three different profiles, which had been manipulated to reflect varying levels of similarity to the subject. If the researcher uses a different set of subjects for each level of similarity (independent groups), three times as many subjects would be needed.

The danger in using repeated measures is that participation in one condition may alter participation in another.

The danger in using repeated measures is that participation in one condition may alter participation in another. For instance, suppose the independent variable had been strength of fear appeal (e.g., strong, moderate, and mild). If the manipulation had involved altering the severity of consequences or a situation in three versions of the same message, it would not have been sensible to use the same subjects in all three conditions. The second and third times the subjects heard the message, they would be aware of the nature of the manipulation and, therefore, would not process the rest of the information as if they were hearing it for the first time. This problem could be surmounted by using three entirely different messages. However, the researcher would then need either to ensure that the messages did not differ in any other important feature or to use a larger number of subjects so that each basic message was combined with each level of fear appeal and presented to a different group of subjects.

In the latter case, the researcher has failed to conserve subjects, but has enhanced the external generalizability of the study by using three messages. At any rate, if the researcher wishes to use repeated measures, it is necessary to ensure that doing so does not bias the performance of the subjects in some conditions.

DETERMINING SPECIFIC CONDITIONS

In an ideal design, the assignment of each subject to experimental condition(s) would be done individually and randomly. By random assignment of subjects, the researcher avoids any bias that might be introduced by subjects in one condition having different characteristics or experiences from subjects in another. The danger in not using random assignment to experimental conditions is that one group may differ from another on a dimension that is relevant to the dependent variable, thereby contaminating the research.

In practice, random assignment of subjects to conditions is not always possible. When the experimental manipulation must be presented to a group as a whole (a speech to a class, for example), it may not be possible to assign individuals separately to experimental conditions. This creates a problem only if the group has unique characteristics or experiences that might affect its responses. For example, the issue discussed in the speech might have served as a topic for a group discussion in this class. When groups rather than individuals must be assigned to experimental conditions, the best the experimenter can do is to use random assignment of groups and to use a number of groups in each condition.

❑ Humane Treatment of Subjects

In addition to the effort that the researcher invests in protecting the integrity of the design, it is equally important to protect the rights and interests of the individuals who serve as subjects in the project. In general, they should be better off as a result of their participation.

It is not possible to detail here all the kinds of guidelines that typically are used to monitor research involving human subjects. The most encompassing principle a researcher can follow is to treat subjects with the same consideration that all people deserve in any situation.

On a more specific level, the two most common admonitions are the need to avoid deceiving subjects and engaging in activities that might negatively affect their self concepts.

Two or three decades ago it was common to fabricate a rationale offered to subjects as the reason for engaging in the activity central to the study. Not surprisingly, subjects resented this deception when they were later told the true purpose of the study. Moreover, this deceptive practice sometimes introduced unnecessary bias in the results. For example, subjects might have been told that they were being asked to express their opinions on public issues to help select topics for campus forums when, in reality, the researcher's goal was to assess subjects' feelings on sensitive issues, such as racial ones. The assumption was that subjects would be reluctant to express their true feelings if they were told the actual reason for soliciting their opinions. The subjects may have responded, however, not with their own opinions, but rather with what they perceived to be widely held public opinions. To preserve the subjects' right to be dealt with truthfully and to prevent unnecessary bias, most researchers today avoid any kind of deception.

A second crucial feature in the humane treatment of subjects is to avoid damaging their self concepts. You may have read of the classic studies in which individuals were asked to administer shocks to others. Many subjects were greatly disturbed to realize that they had been willing to inflict pain on another individual for the sake of "science."

Many other examples of damage to subjects from participation in research projects exist. Subjects' self concepts have been damaged both by the experimental manipulation itself and by the debriefing which typically follows administration of the study. During *debriefing*, subjects are told the purpose of the study, and why they were asked to do what they did. Imagine that the researcher had been studying the impact of temporary enhancement or deflation of the subject's self concept on attraction to a stranger. Subjects in the deflation condition would have been treated inhumanely, since during the study they would have been told information (perhaps fabricated) designed to lower their self concepts. Subjects in the enhancement condition also would have been treated inhumanely. Although they received flattering information during the study itself, they would have learned during debriefing that this information had been contrived. They would then realize that the flattering information was either fabricated or not spontaneous, and moreover, they might then feel very gullible and naive for having initially believed it. The researcher should attempt to anticipate the impact that participation in the study could have on subjects and take precautions to avoid damaging the self concepts of the subjects.

In addition to avoiding negative impact on subjects, the researcher should attempt to make participation in a study a positive experience for subjects. In most communication research, subjects receive no monetary compensation for their efforts. Typically they have donated their time to the researcher's project.

The researcher can, however, make participation in a research project a learning experience for the subjects. During debriefing the researcher should discuss the general nature of the project, the importance of this line of work, and the potential contribution of this specific project. Subjects also appreciate learning applications of such a project to aspects of their own lives. Thus one important decision the researcher should make in preparing a project is how to present it to subjects in the manner that will be most meaningful to them.

❑ Subject Orientation

Principles guiding the treatment of subjects have been influenced in recent years by awareness that subjects are not passive respondents. In fact, the orientation and assumptions that subjects bring to a study have the potential to influence the results.

Moreover, the way they are treated in the research setting may influence this orientation.

Researchers can take steps to evaluate subject apprehension that has the potential to bias results.

The orientation or role subjects assume in a study has itself been studied. In a classic paper, Weber and Cook (1972) identified four roles or orientations that subjects assume. Participants may be *faithful* subjects, simply following instructions without regard to what the hypothesis might be. They may be *good* subjects who attempt to discern the hypothesis and to confirm it. They may be *negativistic* subjects, individuals who attempt to identify the hypothesis in order to sabotage it. Or they may be *apprehensive* subjects, concerned about how they will be evaluated rather than about the hypothesis.

Although not all subjects adopt one of these roles consistently, many individuals behave like apprehensive subjects, concerned primarily about the way in which they will be evaluated personally. This seems plausible, since most of us are continually concerned about how we are being evaluated.

If the researcher understands this apprehension, it usually is possible to avoid letting it bias the results. For instance, a researcher investigating prejudices might worry that subjects will be reluctant to express their true feelings for fear of giving a socially undesirable response. In such a case the researcher might devise a procedure that would permit subjects to remain totally anonymous. In a study of strategies that subjects use when dealing with conflict, subjects' apprehension might lead them to assume that the experimenter evaluates some approaches more positively than others. This could result in subjects' conceding to others more than they normally would in such a circumstance. In this case, the researcher might emphasize that there is no such thing as a correct or proper approach, and that there is real interest in the way in which people deal with similar situations in everyday life.

In general, researchers can take steps to reduce evaluation apprehension that has potential to bias results. Ensuring anonymity, when it is possible, is one such step. Reassuring subjects about the acceptability of any sincere response is another. Emphasizing that responses will be analyzed to determine how groups of people rather than individuals behave sometimes relieves apprehension. Even referring to the enterprise as a project rather than as an experiment may help to diminish anxiety. In any project, the researcher should anticipate the locus of apprehension and deal with it.

❑ Study Questions

Divide into groups of four and discuss the following:

1. What is the ideal relationship between a sample and a population.
2. When a researcher must rely on subjects who happen to be available rather than those who are ideally available, to what kind of population can the results be generalized?
3. What is the difference between an independent groups and repeated measures design? What are the advantages and limitations of each?
4. How does assignment of subjects to the conditions of a study have the potential to influence the results of the study?
5. What is meant by humane treatment of subjects?
6. How does the orientation of the subjects have the potential to influence the results of the study?
7. Think of a study you have read in which the evaluation apprehension of the subjects might have influenced the results of the study.

7

Evaluating a Dependent Measure

An experiment may have more than one dependent variable, but it always has at least one. The measuring instrument selected to assess each dependent variable should possess three critical attributes: reliability, validity, and utility. The *reliability* of an instrument refers to the replicability or stability of scores obtained using the measure. The *validity* of an instrument indicates the degree to which the instrument actually measures the concept it was designed to assess. And the *utility* of an instrument reflects the extent to which the instrument can provide full and insightful information regarding how the variable operates.

It should be emphasized that instruments are not reliable, valid, and/or useful in a vacuum. Rather, these attributes are relevant to a specific purpose. Thus an instrument might be reliable, valid, and useful for one purpose, but not for another. For instance, standard credibility scales may be reliable, valid, and useful for assessing the impact of speaker credibility on immediate attitude change following exposure to a persuasive message, but not for indexing the effects of different instructional styles on ratings of teachers' effectiveness. The reason for this is that dimensions of judgment that lead to a person being considered persuasive may differ from those that are related to effective teaching. For example, being sympathetic to students' needs may be important in evaluating teacher's effectiveness but not in judging persuasive speakers.

The researcher should document the reliability, validity, and utility of the measuring instrument(s) used. This may be done by using evidence from prior research or by providing evidence obtained in the current context. Since it is crucial that the instrument(s) used in a study be reliable, valid, and useful, we will discuss ways of enhancing and assessing these attributes of a measuring instrument. If you plan to be a consumer of research rather than an active participant, you need not try to remember all of the procedures discussed as ways of achieving the three attributes of a good instrument. Understanding the general underlying processes will aid your assessment of the research reports you encounter.

❑ Reliability

THE NATURE OF RELIABILITY

As mentioned above, the reliability of an instrument refers to the degree to which it produces stable or replicable scores. That is, if the phenomenon being assessed has not changed, an instrument is reliable to the extent that it produces the same score with multiple administrations. Suppose that you measure a sofa for a slip cover and decide to measure it a second time to ensure your accuracy. The more similar the two sets of measurements are, the more reliable they are said to be.

Unreliability can be a function of a number of factors. In the case of measuring the sofa for instance, the tape measure might not have been held taut, it might have been placed slightly past the end of the sofa during one measurement, or the person doing the measuring might have read the tape from a different angle each time.

Similarly, any communication measure is susceptible to threats of unreliability from a variety of sources. Suppose that you wished to assess the degree to which male versus female participants in a problem-solving group discussion make supportive statements. The scoring procedure would involve isolating each statement and coding it into categories designed to reflect the supportiveness of the statement. Unreliability could arise from a number of factors. For instance, two coders might disagree regarding where the boundaries between statements occur, or the same coder might not make a consistent judgment on this matter at two different times. In the same way, two coders might differ regarding the way that a particular statement ought to be coded, or again, a single coder might not be consistent in this judgment. Moreover, even if coders are consistent in the judgments, we must assume that subjects likewise are consistent in their behavior. In other words, we must assume that the specific discussion being coded accurately reflects the general level of supportiveness that men and women display in problem-solving discussions.

The researcher must make two types of decisions regarding the reliability: first, what steps to take to ensure that reliability is as high as possible, and, second, what procedure to use to assess reliability.

ENHANCING RELIABILITY

To produce the highest reliability, the researcher must attempt to anticipate potential threats to reliability and guard against them. For example, the researcher should provide careful definitions both for boundaries of statements and categories of supportiveness. These definitions should have been refined by asking coders to apply them, then identifying the instances in which coders failed to reach consistent judgments, followed by reworking the definitions so that coders could apply them once more. This process should continue until consistent responses are obtained. In addition, the researcher could collect a number of problem-solving discussions and have samples of each coded to ensure that the primary discussion being coded typified the supportive behavior of men and women. If it does not, the researcher might elect to use a different discussion or to use segments of a variety of discussions.

ASSESSING RELIABILITY

Once the researcher has taken measures to enhance reliability, it then is appropriate to assess reliability so that the reader of the report is satisfied that it is sufficiently high. Needless to say, if reliability is low, we cannot have faith in the results, because if the study were replicated, we might find something quite different.

What serves as an assessment of reliability varies from case to case, in terms of both what is being assessed and the method of assessment. Typically what is reported is a measure reflecting the agreement between scores on the dependent measure. For example, in the illustration outlined above, the reliability coefficient most likely would reflect the degree of agreement between the two coders' final scores. If the data permit, the reliability coefficient most likely would be some form of correlation coefficient. If the data cannot be treated in this manner, the assessment of reliability might indicate the percentage of exact agreement in the codings of the two raters.

Clearly the most important decisions the researcher makes regarding reliability are those that enhance the consistency of the measure. However, it is also important to demonstrate the effectiveness with which this has been done by reporting a reliability coefficient.

❑ Validity

THE NATURE OF VALIDITY

An instrument is valid to the extent that it measures what it is designed to measure. A measure cannot have high validity without high reliability, because it cannot truly assess what it was designed to unless it produces consistent scores. However, high reliability does not guarantee high validity. It is possible for an instrument to produce scores that are consistent but do not bear a strong relationship to what the instrument is presumed to measure.

Consider again the question of supportiveness displayed in a group discussion. The researcher might define the category encompassing supportiveness to include all statements that indicate any merit in the idea expressed. Thus the following statement might be classified as supportive: "That's a pretty good idea, but I feel that proposal has far more risks than some people realize." The speaker may then elaborate a number of problems embedded in the proposal. Perhaps the researcher's original conception of support was broad enough to encompass the statement just cited. On the other hand, the researcher may have intended support to mean encouraging agreement with the position of another. In that case, such a statement would not fit the definition, and if it were classified as supportive, this would be a source of validity.

It is important to avoid confusing the concept of the validity of a measuring instrument with the concepts of the internal and external validity of a design. Recall that the internal validity of a design refers to the validity of drawing conclusions based on *all* the procedures used in the design. And external validity refers to the extent to which the conclusions from a given study can legitimately be generalized to other contexts. Both internal and external validity refer to characteristics of the whole design. By contrast, the validity of a measuring instrument is a more limited concern; it refers specifically to the extent to which the instrument accurately assesses the attribute it was designed to measure.

STEPS IN DEVELOPING AND VALIDATING AN INSTRUMENT

If the researcher wishes to develop a valid procedure for measuring a particular variable, it is essential to begin with a clear conception of that variable. The researcher must analyze what the crucial features of the variable are and how they are manifested or reflected in ways that might be directly observed.

Consider the method used by one researcher in developing an instrument that he hoped would be a valid measure of source credibility. Berlo, Lemert, and Mertz (1969-1970), in their early work on credibility, defined credibility as those judgments made about a source that influence the ability of that source to persuade others to a particular point of view. Clearly not all of the judgments that we make about a source of a message are relevant to the believability of that person. For instance, we might notice that the individual gestured more with the left hand than with the right, but it is unlikely that this dimension of judgment would affect our reaction to the message.

Thus in order to discover just what dimensions of judgment actually do affect our inclination to believe a source, Berlo and colleagues asked a large number of individuals to indicate the traits of sources that affected their willingness to believe a message from those sources. In this way Berlo et al. empirically derived the attributes of sources relevant to their believability.

Next the researchers devised scales designed to assess these fundamental traits. They selected semantic differential scales (i.e., scales that take the form of a seven-unit scale bounded by polar adjectives). For instance, some of the scales they used are these:

intelligent	___ ___ ___ ___ ___ ___ ___	unintelligent
experienced	___ ___ ___ ___ ___ ___ ___	inexperienced
trained	___ ___ ___ ___ ___ ___ ___	untrained

Researchers using such scales typically sum responses across more than one scale designed to measure the same attribute, such as expertise, to yield a more stable or reliable measure. In the case of the credibility scales, responses to the scales on experience, intelligence, and training were summed, along with other similar types of scales. Thus if a subject interprets any one scale in an idiosyncratic way, the subject's score on the concept (such as expertise) will not be unduly biased.

Subsequent researchers took the next important step in validating these measures of credibility. They demonstrated that the attributes measured by these scales were actually related to the believability of a message. Thus if one source scored higher than another on the attribute of expertise, then the source with the higher score also was likely to generate a more positive attitude in listeners toward the proposition contained in a message. The standard procedure used was to present the same message to two different audiences, but to manipulate perceptions of the credibility of the source. For instance, in a speech urging greater use of contraceptives as a means of controlling venereal disease, one audience might be told that the source was an official from The Center for Disease Control, whereas the other audience might be told that the source was a college freshman fulfilling a speech requirement. The researcher would then compare the degree of belief generated by each source. (As a manipulation check, the researcher also would verify that one source scored higher on the credibility scales than did the other.) In this way, the researcher could document that the credibility scales actually reflected what they were designed to measure (i.e., attributes that affect the believability of a source).

Thus the fundamental procedure for developing an instrument is to (1) identify clearly the central features of the variable to be measured, (2) devise a method for observing variations in these features, and (3) verify that the method of observation does, in fact, assess those features of the variable it was designed to tap. The researcher must either execute these procedures or document the effectiveness of these procedures from prior work. The third step in this process is the validation process. This step ensures that the instrument truly does assess the variable it was intended to assess.

METHODS OF VALIDATING AN INSTRUMENT

A variety of procedures are available to assess the validity of an instrument. We might point out that some procedures, although labeled validation procedures, do not directly assess the extent to which an instrument measures what it was designed to assess. For instance, *face validity* refers to the extent to which an instrument appears to measure what it was designed to assess. Sometimes it is desirable for the instrument to appear to measure a certain variable, particularly if a group that must approve its use is skeptical about the value of an instrument. (For example, if a school system wishes to use an achievement test, parents may be more agreeable if the test looks as though it measures the skills in question.)

At other times, it may be undesirable for an instrument to have face validity. If the researcher wishes to withhold the real purpose of the study, perhaps because of concern that the desire to provide socially acceptable responses will bias the outcome, then it may be preferable to use an instrument that does not reveal the variable of interest. For instance, suppose the researcher were studying whether faculty or students held more biased attitudes toward members of racial minorities. If it was obvious that biased attitudes were being measured, individuals might not respond truthfully. In this case an instrument with low face validity would be preferable. In either case, however, face validity is concerned only with what an instrument appears to measure, not with what it actually does measure.

In similar fashion, content validity does not directly reflect the extent to which an instrument assesses what it was designed to measure. Rather, *content validity* indicates the extent to which an instrument is an adequate sampling of a whole domain of variables to be measured. It is not applicable, therefore, to instances in which a researcher is trying to assess a single, unidimensional variable. Content validity is relevant only when many variables are to be assessed within a single instrument. For instance, an instructor constructing a final examination must consider whether the examination adequately samples from all concepts to be evaluated in the final examination. But again, this in no way guarantees that a specific item truly assesses the concept it is designed to measure.

By contrast, convergent validity offers at least some indication that an instrument is valid. *Convergent validity* refers to the extent to which scores on the measure in question correspond to those on another measure that is designed to assess the same concept and already known to have some validity. Needless to say, the latter condition makes use of convergent validity somewhat limited. It can be used only when a valid measure for the same concept already exists. For example, the researcher might be developing an instrument that is easier to use than one already employed, but aimed at tapping the same concept.

The two procedures that offer perhaps the most direct support for the validity of an instrument are criterion and construct validity. *Criterion validity* indicates the extent to which an instrument reflects the actual behavior (the criterion) it is designed to assess. (You may read of concurrent or predictive validity, which are subcategories of criterion validity.)

Consider an example of criterion validity. Admission to many academic programs requires students to take a standardized examination. The Graduate Record Examination (GRE), for instance, is designed to assess potential to do well at graduate work. If you define doing well as making good grades in graduate level courses, then it would be possible to compare students' scores on the GRE with the grade point averages they compiled in graduate level courses. The grade point average is the criterion in this case. A strong relationship between GRE scores and students' grade point averages is a good indication of the degree to which the instrument measures the variable it was intended to tap. Unfortunately, in communication research, behavioral criteria such as the one described in this example are seldom available.

The most common procedure for validating instruments used in communication research is construct validity. *Construct validity* involves deriving testable principles involving the variable to be assessed where the principles would readily be granted by reasonable people, then using the instrument to test the principles, and assuming that any difficulties encountered in supporting the principles suggest problems with the validity of the instrument rather than with the principles themselves. In other words, the procedure involved in construct validation is the inverse of that used in an experiment. In an experiment, a study is conducted using a measuring instrument assumed to be valid in order to determine whether a principle or hypothesis is true. In construct validation, a study is conducted in order to determine whether the instrument is capable of verifying a principle or hypothesis *already* assumed to be true. If the study fails to offer support for the principle, rather than concluding that the hypothesis is false, the instrument is assumed to lack validity.

An example may serve to clarify the process of construct validation. Daniel O'Keefe and Howard Sypher (1981) compared the construct validity of several measures of the level of differentiation of an individual's interpersonal construct system with a detailed comparison of the two most commonly used measures. The level of differentiation of an individual's interpersonal construct system refers to the number of dimensions of judgment an individual uses when perceiving other people. For example, a person with a restricted interpersonal construct system might perceive people primarily along only two dimensions: how nice they are and how interesting they are. Other individuals, with more elaborated interpersonal construct systems, might employ far more dimensions of perception. For instance, in addition to considering how nice and interesting people are, they might perceive people in terms of their sense of social responsibility, their desire to please others, and their willingness to defend others unrightfully attacked, among other things.

O'Keefe and Sypher identified several principles derived from our understanding of an individual's personal construct system that most reasonable people would assume to be true. First, as children mature, their interpersonal construct systems typically become more elaborated. Second, the degree of elaboration of an individual's construct system is related to other social cognitive skills, such as the ability to understand the perspective of other individuals. Third, the degree of differentiation of an individual's interpersonal construct system bears some relationship to the level of skill an individual displays in communication tasks, and so forth. O'Keefe and Sypher compared the two primary measures of differentiation to determine which offered better support for these principles. One provided consistent support for all the principles, whereas the other did not. Since these principles were already thought to be true, the comparison served to assess the measuring instruments rather than hypotheses. Consequently, O'Keefe and Sypher concluded that the measure that offered consistent support for these principles had greater construct validity. (This measure, incidentally, was the Role Category Questionnaire, a measure that indicates the number of attributes an individual uses to describe others whom the individual knows well by counting the number of attributes used to describe others.)

As you can see, documenting the validity of a measuring instrument can be a very complicated task. For this reason, researchers frequently rely on instruments whose validity has already been established rather than engaging in the laborious process of devising and validating a new one.

❑ Utility

THE NATURE OF UTILITY

Because demonstrating the reliability and validity of an instrument is so demanding, it is tempting to rely on well-developed instruments without adequate concern for the final criterion for selection of a measuring procedure, its utility. A measure is useful to the extent that it gives the richest and fullest picture of the variable under consideration. Just as a measure may be reliable and valid for one purpose but not another, so a measure may be more useful for one purpose than another. Unlike reliability and validity, however, there are no systematic procedures to follow that ensure utility of a measure. What we can suggest, however, are guidelines that serve to help the researcher select or develop measures that yield measures of more utility than others.

DISPLAYS FULL RANGE OF RESPONSES

Useful instruments are capable of displaying the full range of responses that subjects might make. You may have had the experience of attempting to complete a survey only to discover that you are forced to choose among responses when none of the alternatives reflects your real view. Such an instrument cannot possibly capture the full range of responses that subjects might make. For example, suppose you were asked to indicate your favorite dessert, but were given only three options: carrot cake, lemon pie, and chocolate mousse. If your favorite dessert is mocha chip ice cream, you would find the instrument frustrating, and your response would be misleading.

Structured responses (i.e., those that specify the range of possible alternatives for subjects) are obviously subject to the potential danger of failing to adequately represent the full range of actual responses. (It should be noted, however, that careful pretesting can help enormously in surmounting this problem.)

Even when subjects are permitted to express their responses fully in an open-ended fashion (in the case above, to write down their favorite dessert), the potential for failing to adequately *display* the full range of responses still exists. In this case, however, the problem arises when the researcher attempts to categorize the responses, since the category system itself may fail to reflect the total range of responses. It might be possible to summarize favorite desserts without violating the original meaning of the responses. But imagine a more complicated kind of response that one might get in a study of communication behavior. Suppose the researcher were studying the features of a message individuals use to terminate a romantic relationship. Subjects might be asked to write down everything they said to their partner at the time they let the partner know they wished to end the relationship. If there were 500 subjects, it would be impossible to reproduce what might be thousands of pages of messages in a research report. The researcher would be forced to construct a category system that hopefully would reflect the key features contained in the responses.

The researcher could begin by constructing a preliminary set of categories based on careful reading of a subset of messages, and then having other coders attempt to categorize a different set of the messages using this category system. If high reliability were achieved, we would have assurance that at least the categories could be used consistently.

The system might, however, not capture the most useful features of the system. Remember that what is useful depends on the purpose motivating the study. Imagine further that the researcher's underlying motivation is to discover features of messages terminating relationships that predict whether the jilted partner will maintain positive feelings toward the person ending the relationship. Validity could be assessed by comparing the way messages had been categorized with some actual assessment of the jilted partner's feelings (assuming it were possible to gain cooperation from individuals who actually had been jilted and also to have access to the kinds of messages their former partners had used to end the relationship).

Determining the utility of the category system would be more difficult. The coding scheme might reliably and validly distinguish among messages that expressed positive, neutral, and negative feelings toward the jilted party. (For example, "I still think you're the most wonderful person I know" would be categorized as positive, whereas "You just don't seem like the same wonderful person I fell in love with" would be categorized as negative.) But statements expressing explicit feelings toward the jilted partner might not be the only message features that influenced the jilted partners' feelings. For instance, another relevant feature might be whether the person ending the relationship cited external reasons for terminating the relationship. If this person mentioned factors such as pressure from family to avoid commitment or the need to spend more time on work, the jilted partner might also feel less negatively toward the former partner. The most useful category system, then, would be one that represented the full range of features in the messages that influenced the feelings of the jilted partner.

There is no procedure that guarantees such a system, although there are procedures that increase the likelihood of its development. For example, after the researcher had extracted from the message all the features that seemed relevant to him or her, the researcher could invite a number of other individuals to scrutinize the messages in an attempt to identify features that they saw as potentially relevant to the feelings of the jilted partner. Better yet, the researcher could conduct extensive interviews with some of the jilted partners to see what aspects of their partners' messages they mentioned as affecting their feelings. It is crucial, however, that the researcher exert effort to ensure that all of the relevant features of the response are represented in the coding system.

PROVIDES INSIGHT INTO RATIONALE FOR BEHAVIOR

In general, research is more useful when it offers insight into the reason why a phenomenon occurs. Thus in social scientific research, a second guideline for assessing the utility of a dependent measure is the degree to which it offers insight into the rationale for behavior.

Consider a line of research in which understanding the rationale for behavior has proved particularly useful. In much of the work on selection of message strategies, researchers have relied on the procedure of presenting subjects with hypothetical but realistic situations and asking them what they would say. For example, children have been asked what they would say if they were attempting to persuade their mother to let them have an overnight party. Messages then are coded into categories ordered by some underlying principle. For the example just cited, messages were coded for the degree to which they accommodated to the needs and wants of the persuadee (Clark & Delia, 1976). Hence the major categories, ordered from the least to the most accommodative, were (1) no justification for request, (2) justification in terms of the needs and wants of the persuader, (3) response to the counterarguments of the persuadee, and (4) offering direct benefit to the persuadee.

As researchers used this coding scheme, it became apparent that some individuals were capable of using an advanced level strategy (offering advantage to the other) but elected to use a lower level appeal instead (stressing their own needs or wants), A little girl who was trying to persuade her father to buy a new bike mentioned that she could have told him that having a new bike would mean that she could ride to school and he would not need to drive her. But she chose to say, instead, that all her friends had ten-speed bikes and that she really wanted one also. When pressed for the reason for this choice, she said that she knew that her father really enjoyed doing nice things for her, and she felt sure she would get the bike if he thought she really wanted it. Cases such as this made it clear that the coding scheme being used was a valid measure of how a person would behave in a specific situation, but probably did not reflect the potential for the kinds of messages the individual was capable of using.

Since researchers were interested in the subject's *potential* to accommodate messages to others' needs and wants, it was necessary to develop a measure of the subject's rationale for selecting message strategies. As a consequence, after subjects produced a message, researchers (Burke & Clark, 1982) began asking them what had led them to develop it in the manner in which they did. A new coding scheme was devised to classify these rationales for the degree to which they reflected an understanding of the other's perspective. As you can see, understanding the rationale for an individual's behavior is more critical to some research questions than to others.

POTENTIAL FOR SERENDIPITY

Some measuring instruments provide more information than is directly sought by the researcher and thus have the potential to provide unexpected insights regarding the nature of the variable under consideration.

Consider an illustration. A number of years ago I was studying the kinds of message strategies an individual might use to congratulate a person who had recently had good fortune despite the fact that the good fortune seemed undeserved. For instance, I asked college students what they would say to congratulate a classmate who had just been offered a job that the subject also had interviewed for and seemed better qualified for. Some students replied that they simply would not congratulate the classmate. So next I changed the instructions slightly and simply asked what the student would say to the classmate. In this way I was able to discover the full range of responses students would make. For instance, I discovered that some students saw this as an opportunity to gain valuable information. Hence their response might be something like: "That's great that you got the position with Megabucks. What kinds of things did you stress in your interview that you think led to their hiring you?" Others felt that the undeserved good fortune ought to be belittled, and their reply went something like this: "Well I hope it all works out for you. I've heard that Megabucks is really in transition now." Others simply wanted to make the classmate feel good and used a conventional response. Thus their reply might be. "I'm really happy for you. That's a great opportunity and you really deserve it." Clearly individuals defined their objectives in constructing a message in this situation quite differently. It was essential to phrase the question put to them in a way that allowed for a range of responses and then to develop a coding system to display this range. Coupled with questions regarding the rationale for their responses, this led to a much fuller understanding of the situation than I had upon entering the project.

Measuring instruments that allow subjects to structure their own responses frequently have greater potential for the kinds of serendipitous findings just described. But even structured measuring instruments have such potential. In this case, the researcher needs to be especially sensitive to responses that deviate markedly from what was initially expected. At times a pattern will emerge in these responses that will enable the researcher to rethink the issue in question.

By now it should be apparent that facilitating and assessing the reliability, validity, and utility of a measuring instrument is a complex matter. The consumer of research should keep these characteristics of measuring instruments in mind when evaluating the report of any investigation.

❏ Study Questions

Divide into groups of four and answer the following:

1. What is meant by the reliability of a measuring instrument?
2. Describe how you might assess the reliability of these instruments: (a) a seven-point scale to assess liking and (b) the coding of the statements in an argument into five categories (assertion of own position, attempt to understand position of other, attempt to find compromise, attempt to blame other for disagreement, attempt to change topic).
3. What is meant by validity? Why is it important?
4. Consider a scale for assessing liking in which subjects are asked to respond to the statement, I like person X very much.

Agree strongly	Agree moderately	Agree somewhat	Disagree somewhat	Disagree moderately	Disagree strongly

    a. To what extent does the instrument have face validity?

    b. If you wanted to use a criterion validation procedure with this scale, what might you do?

    c. If you wanted to use a construct validation procedure with this scale, what might you do?

5. Suppose you wanted to measure liking for a stranger with whom the subject had a brief encounter. In addition to using the scale just described, you might also ask the subject to write a paragraph describing things he or she liked and disliked about the other person. In what way might this elicit more useful information than that contained in the scale itself?

Types of Dependent Measures

It is important that a dependent measuring instrument be reliable and valid and provide useful information. In studying interpersonal communication, there is a wide range of types of measuring instruments, and at times the researcher may need to make a choice among several types of instruments designed to measure the same variable. For instance, communication apprehension has been assessed by self reports (an individual's report of how apprehensive he or she felt in a particular situation), by observer reports of the apprehension exhibited by the individual, and by measurement of the physiological reactions of the individual while speaking (by means of galvanic skin response).

Consequently, we will discuss some of the alternative types of measures available and the unique advantages and limitations each offers as a dependent measure. We will consider first measures designed to assess some feature of overt behavior and then measures intended to reflect some internal state of the individual. This discussion does not encompass all of the approaches that are available to the researcher studying interpersonal communication, but includes a number of commonly used approaches.

❏ Measures of Behavior

CONDITIONS UNDER WHICH DATA ARE GATHERED

Behavior Obtained as It Occurs Naturally and Without the Knowledge of the Subject

It is important to know whether the subject is aware of being observed or evaluated. When the subject knows that he or she is being observed, the subject's behavior may be altered. It is natural for individuals to want to make a favorable impression on others, and on themselves as well; thus people may alter their behavior (perhaps unconsciously) when they think they are the object of scrutiny. Changes in behavior occur even when the individuals are not certain what dimension of their behavior is being evaluated. For example, imagine that you have been visiting with a friend in a public but deserted area and think that you are alone, but then discover that someone has been sitting the entire time within hearing range. You may feel a bit uncomfortable in a case like this even when you don't know the other individual and likely will never see this person again. This feeling of apprehension is magnified considerably if you discover that you are being observed for a research project and that your behavior is being carefully scrutinized, even if you do not know the dimension on which your behavior is being evaluated.

Therefore, for some purposes, to ensure that subjects will behave in a completely natural manner, researchers use approaches to measurement in which subjects are never aware that they are participating in a study. Recall Burgoon and Aho's

(1982) study of the violation of interpersonal distance (i.e., standing unusually close or far away from each other) on the nonverbal behavior of the other person. The researchers had confederates pose as customers pretending to be interested in buying an item in a store and standing at one of three distances (normal, close, or far) from the clerk. Two additional members of the research team then observed and recorded the nonverbal behavior of the salesperson, who was the subject in the study. The clerk never knew that he or she was participating in the study. This procedure was repeated until sufficient number of clerks to constitute an adequate subject sample had been observed.

The primary advantage of such a procedure is observing behavior as it actually occurs. For instance, if the clerks had known they were being observed, they might have been less likely to display signs of discomfort when the customer stood either too close or too far away.

The disadvantage, however, is that the behavior is fleeting, and it might not always be possible to obtain an accurate record of the behavior. In the study described above, the clerk did not know that a study was being conducted. Thus the clerk might have moved in such a fashion that the observers would have had difficulty seeing clearly. The observers had no permanent record of the behavior, such as a videotape, which might have been possible if the subjects had known they were participating in a study.

Subject Knows Behavior Observed, but Does not Know Variable of Interest

At times the individuals involved in a study know that their behavior is being observed, but they may not know that they are participating in a research project, and even if they do, they do not know its purpose or the variable of interest. For instance, a researcher might obtain permission to have access to videotapes of city council discussions, but the discussants would have no knowledge of what use was to be made of the tapes. It is hoped that such a procedure would have many of the same advantages of the study of naturalistic behavior described in the preceding section. This would be likely to be true if the discussants normally were videotaped for other reasons.

If the videotaping were not typical, the researcher might take precautions to make it seem more natural in order to avoid altering the ordinary behavior of the discussants. For instance, the camera should be located unobtrusively and the researcher might videotape at least two discussions before taping the one that will be analyzed so that the participants would no longer be thinking about the videotaping.

Once the record of behavior exists, a series of videotapes in this case, they can be coded to reflect one or more of a variety of dependent measures. One might code the tapes to describe the direction of interaction (e.g., who talks to whom). Or one might use categories to describe the kinds of comments that are made such as offering information, evaluating positions of others, and seeking information. Or one could focus particular interactants and note whether their comments tend to be dominant or submissive. Obviously the measure used would be entirely contingent on the variable of interest to the researcher and the researcher's assessment of the reliability and validity of the measure.

Behavior Deliberately Generated to Be Observed

The behavior described thus far would occur regardless of whether research was being conducted. There are even more times, however, when conducting a research project, that individuals are asked to perform behavior specifically for the purpose of the study. In such cases, subjects usually, although not always, realize they are participating in research. (The behavior might be integrated into class activities so that subjects are unaware that a research project is involved.) Frequently, however, subjects know that they are being asked to engage in behavior for research purposes, but have no idea what aspect of the behavior is of interest. They may be asked to role play situations of the sort the researcher would like to observe. For example, if a researcher interested in group behavior had been unable to study naturally occurring discussions, he or she might have asked groups of students or other individuals to engage in discussions of certain kinds. In fact, more of the literature on group discussions is based on this kind of behavior than on naturally occurring group discussions.

Similarly, the literature in persuasion has relied heavily on analysis of behavior generated specifically for the purposes of research. Subjects typically are given a specific situation, which might occur, and asked what they would say.

The success of this approach of generating behavior specifically for the purposes of analysis depends on how closely this behavior approximates behavior that occurs naturally in similar circumstances. There are precautions the researcher can take to attempt to elicit naturalistic behavior. For instance, researchers may pretest the kinds of situations that the individuals will be asked to respond to in order to select ones that the subjects find realistic. In a persuasive task, for example, the researcher might use a pretest that asks subjects to indicate whether they can imagine themselves in such a circumstance.

Sometimes the researcher will structure the situation to enhance the naturalism of the behavior elicited. In a persuasive situation, the researcher might offer an incentive to the subjects to convince the other individual as a means of increasing their desire to persuade the other individual. Bearison and Gass (1979) offered children a monetary reward if they succeeded in persuading another child to their view. One criticism sometimes leveled at the research in group discussion is that participants are not greatly concerned with the outcome of the discussion. If this is the case, participants might appear more accommodating than they actually would be if the outcome had serious personal consequences. Incentives could be used to increase participant involvement.

At times the research task can be embedded in a context that disguises the purpose of the task. In studying the conversational involvement of lonely people, Bell (1985) left a lonely person (identified earlier by an inventory) with a partner for 10 minutes and asked them to get acquainted until the experimenter returned. The videotaped conversation that occurred provided one source of data for the study, but participants may have assumed that the "real" study would begin as soon as the researcher returned. Following the conversation, the individuals were separated and asked questions that served as an additional source of data for the study.

Selecting from Preformulated Alternative Behaviors

In all the examples of behavior cited so far, the subject produced a specimen of behavior, even if only through role playing. Another technique of observing behavior does not call for the subject to generate the behavior, but rather asks the subject to designate from a set of descriptions or preformulated behaviors which one(s) he or she would be most likely to use in a given situation.

Much of the research in compliance gaining has been conducted using this approach. Subjects are given a specific situation and then asked to indicate which items in a set of strategies (persuasive appeals) they would be likely to use in that situation. Marwell and Schmitt (1967) devised the original set of compliance gaining strategies, although it has been modified by a number of other researchers.

Some critics question whether the subjects actually know which strategies they really would use. In particular, the claim has been made that subjects may select more socially desirable responses when they see how they might function rather than less socially desirable ones that they might generate spontaneously (Clark, 1979). There are ways to minimize this effect, however. For instance, the researcher might ask the subject to mentally construct the message he or she might use before selecting from the preformulated list of strategies.

Moreover, there are advantages to selection from preformulated lists that may justify their use. Selection procedures save time for both the subject and the researcher. This makes it possible to increase the sample size as well as the number of situations the subject can respond to. The savings of time to the researcher is enormous, since coding messages can be very time consuming. Selection procedures may yield insight into differences in responses by subjects to alternative situations, even if they risk overestimating the use of socially desirable strategies.

Selection from preformulated behavior has been used for other purposes as well. In studying interpersonal problem-solving styles, Witteman (1988) had participants think about a current problem they were experiencing or about one they had experienced recently. Participants then completed a questionnaire, indicating the likelihood of usage of a series of problem-solving behaviors: For example, "I shared with the other my feelings and thoughts about the problem," "I changed the topic of the discussion away from the issue of the problem," or "I threatened to end the conversation." Such a procedure makes it possible to gather and code a substantial amount of data.

THE NATURE OF THE OBSERVATION OF THE BEHAVIOR

Regardless of how the behavior occurs, the nature of the observation of the behavior can vary widely. One major distinction is whether the researcher has some permanent record of the behavior itself (e.g., a videotape, diary report, or written message) or must find a means of coding the behavior as it transpires. Needless to say, it is usually possible to do more detailed analyses of behavior when a record is available. The record makes it possible to code multiple dimensions of the behavior as well as to check the reliability of the codings. For instance, if one had a videotape of a group discussion, and the primary interest were in charting which members of the discussion seemed to be the focus of attention, it would be possible to code for number of comments directed toward each person, length of comment, and number of people looking at each individual during the comment. It would be more difficult to code this many features of the interaction as the discussion transpired.

When a record is to be made of the behavior, the researcher should consider in advance to how it is to be obtained. A videotape made from one angle might be more valuable than one made from another, for instance. When no record is to be made, it is also important to consider in advance how the behavior is to be coded. Thinking back to the study conducted by Burgoon and Aho (1982), in which the behavior of clerks was observed when customers stood at varying distances from them, you can see the importance of rehearsing in advance where the observers should stand and in what form the behavior should be coded in order to produce reliable and useful accounts of the clerk's behavior.

HOW THE DATA ARE CODED

When behavior is observed, regardless of how it occurs or is recorded, perhaps the most crucial question faced by the researcher is how the behavior is to be coded. Except in the case in which subjects designate which of a set of preformulated behaviors they will perform, the researcher must decide which features of a global behavior to code and what categories to use to represent these features.

The decision is, of course, not a totally unstructured one. The researcher entered the project with a research question or hypothesis that specifies the dependent variable(s) of interest. Assume, for example, that the research question was whether older children when compared to younger children use persuasive strategies that reflect greater understanding of the perspective of the persuadee. The researcher must either find an existing coding system or develop one that assesses the extent to which understanding of the persuadee's perspective is embedded in a persuasive strategy.

In either developing or selecting a coding system, the researcher must, of course, be concerned with the reliability, validity, and utility of the system. For purposes of selecting or developing the coding scheme, the consideration the researcher probably will start with is that of utility. It is crucial to find a system that will offer the most useful information with respect to the hypothesis or research question. Thus there may be a variety of coding schemes available to categorize persuasive strategies, but one is more likely to be more useful than others. For example, some coding schemes for persuasive strategies categorize appeals on the basis of their content (e.g., appeals to money, social needs, or status). Clearly such a scheme would be of little value for the research question at issue, because it ignores the underlying concern of whether the strategy reflects understanding of the needs of the persuadee. The only type of scheme of use to the researcher is one in which the categories can be organized hierarchically to reflect greater understanding of the needs of the persuadee.

Unless information regarding validity is already available, the researcher must assess the validity of the coding scheme.

Once the researcher has either found or developed such a system, it is necessary to be sure that the system can be used with acceptable reliability. To be reliable, it should be possible for *any* individual to take the behavior available (in this case, the persuasive messages generated by the subjects) and code the behavior consistently. If the coding scheme has been developed by others, data should be available regarding its reliability and validity. To achieve such reliability, coders may work with a small subset of the behavior to be analyzed and discuss any differences they may have in their original categorizations. Sometimes more carefully detailed instructions on how to code into certain categories are necessary. After such a training session, the coders may attempt coding another subset of the messages and then again assess their consistency. These steps are repeated until coders reach an acceptable level of agreement concerning the way the behavior should be categorized.

Finally, of course, unless information regarding its validity is already available from other researchers, the researcher must assess the validity of the coding scheme. This is frequently a difficult task. For instance, with the coding scheme described above, there may be no way to know with certainty that the categories reflect increasingly better understanding of the perspective of the persuadee. But the researcher could determine whether a large group of individuals *perceive* the categories as possessing such a characteristic. The means of validation varies widely depending on the nature of the coding scheme.

❏ Assessment of Internal States

We cannot directly observe internal states (e.g., attraction for another, attitudes toward issues, need for inclusion, feelings of satisfaction with a decision). Alternatives available for assessing internal states include physiological measures, inferences of observers, and some form of self-report. Since self-report is the most common type of measure used in communication research, we shall discuss it more fully than the other two.

PHYSIOLOGICAL MEASURES

Physiological measures are not commonly used in studying interpersonal communication and vary widely in their type. Standard physiological measures that have been used in communication research include galvanic skin response (to measure, for instance, communication apprehension) and eye pupil dilation or eye pupil movement (to measure, for example, strong affective reactions, such as attraction toward others or attitudes on an issue).

There are three fundamental problems with physiological measures. First, individuals vary widely in their psychological reactions, regardless of the specific circumstances in which they currently find themselves. Second, it is difficult to really know the internal state responsible for the physiological reaction. Third, the individual usually knows that he or she is being observed (even if not the purpose of the observation), and this may alter the response.

To deal with the first problem, individual variability, researchers commonly establish "baseline" responses for each individual. That is, they assess the physiological response of the individual *prior* to the introduction of the experimental manipulation and then again *after* the manipulation, and use the difference between the two scores as the individual's measure of the impact of the manipulation.

There is no straightforward way of dealing with the second problem, knowing what the physiological response actually indicates in terms of the internal state of the individual. For example, lots of eye pupil movement may reflect a high level of attention on the part of the subject, but it is difficult to be certain whether it is due to a strong positive or a strong negative feeling. One way to validate the link between the physiological response and the attribution of an internal state is through the use of additional techniques. For instance, the researcher might conduct systematic interviews of subjects, asking them to describe their feelings (attitude, attraction, or whatever the variable of interest was) while the researcher noted the physiological response.

It is difficult to deal with the third problem. Usually the subject knows that his or her behavior is being monitored since special equipment frequently is used and the procedure itself may produce some physiological reaction. To counteract this possibility, the subject is sometimes given an opportunity to become somewhat accustomed to the process that is being used.

REPORTS OF OBSERVERS

Ratings of observers designed to reflect the rater's perceptions of the internal state of the subject must be based on external cues. A variable such as communication apprehension (fear of communicating) can be assessed by rater's observations of subjects. But the raters must rely on one or a constellation of behavioral cues (e.g., rapid movements, perspiration, hesitation in speaking, looking around the room, and so on).

The major advantage of using observer ratings is that they are easy to obtain.

The problems with the ratings of external observers are similar in some ways to those of the use of direct behavioral assessments. There are large differences in the nature of the cues produced by certain individuals, and there is no direct way of being certain that the cues observed actually reflect the internal state in question.

Clearly there are likely to be wide individual differences in the cues available to raters to assess a variable such as communication apprehension. Some individuals just naturally move more than others, hesitate more in speaking than others, and look around more than others. It is not easy to establish a normal baseline for each person, since the researcher would need to observe the subjects under widely divergent circumstances to know what is natural for each person.

The second problem, attempting to verify that the cues actually reflect the internal state in question, is potentially quite serious. For example, the manifestations of apprehension may be similar to those of excitement. The researcher might interview subjects and ask them to describe their feelings so that the observed behavior could be linked to reported internal states. Because of these two major problems with observer ratings, it is desirable to use multiple raters and when possible to compare the ratings.

The major advantage of using observer ratings is that they are easy to obtain. Unlike physiological measures, which may require special equipment or training to administer, ratings are usually simple to use. And at times it is possible to observe subjects and make ratings without their knowledge, thereby avoiding social desirability effects (i.e., the tendency to try to "look good"). For instance, it may be possible to observe subjects in their natural environment or with the use of a device such as a one-way mirror. In general, observer ratings are one of the easiest types of data to obtain, and therefore one of the most common, although it is not easy to be sure that they are both reliable and valid.

SELF-REPORTS

In *self-report* measures, the subject describes his or her own feelings or behavior, sometimes with the knowledge of what is being assessed and sometimes without this knowledge. The nature of the report can vary widely. Some of the more common formats are described below.

Diary Accounts

Individuals may be asked to keep a journal or diary of a particular kind of behavior or feeling. For example, studies of moods of teenagers have been conducted by the diary method. Teens have been asked to carry beepers, and at predetermined intervals, the experimenter signals the subjects to record their moods as well as their activity at that moment. From such accounts the researcher can answer questions such as the percentage of time that the subjects experience positive or negative affective states, whether boys differ from girls in their affective states, or whether moods have a direct relationship to the kinds of activities that accompany them.

The primary concern with the diary methodology is whether subjects can accurately assess and report their internal states. Despite these difficulties, the diary method has proved quite useful in a number of areas. For instance, relational communication has been studied by asking individuals to keep a journal of the interactions with their relational partner. The diary method has the advantage of securing substantial amounts of data that otherwise would be inaccessible.

Retrospective Reconstructions

A variation of the diary method is *retrospective reconstruction* in which subjects are asked to produce an account of events that occurred in the past. For instance, subjects might be asked to think of a time when they had ended a romantic relationship. They might then be asked to describe why they desired to end the relationship and to reconstruct as precisely as possible the conversation in which termination of the relationship was discussed.

This methodology presumes that people can produce relatively accurate accounts of past events. Although the accounts provided may be abbreviated and reflect the subject's perspective on the event, they provide a source of data that otherwise would be nearly unattainable.

Projective Tasks

With the use of both diaries and retrospective accounts, the subject has at least a general idea of the experimenter's interest. By contrast, in projective tasks, the subject is asked to perform a task from which the researcher then abstracts information to assess a variable that may not be at all obvious to the subject. One common projective task used in interpersonal communication research is the Role Category Questionnaire. As mentioned earlier, subjects are asked to provide detailed descriptions of peers (usually a close friend and someone they dislike), indicating what kind of person the peer is. From this description the researcher counts the number of nonphysical attributes ascribed to the peers and uses this as an index of the degree of differentiation of the construct system the subject used for perceiving other individuals. Subjects may not know how their descriptions will be analyzed at the time they produce them.

Projective tasks have both advantages and limitations. They should be less susceptible than other measures to the need to provide socially desirable responses unless the subject attempts to guess the purpose of the task. An inaccurate guess could undermine the validity of the measure. For example, a subject might guess that the researcher wanted to know how positively the subjects regarded other people. If the subject therefore omitted all negative constructs, the validity of the measure would be diluted. But in general, projective tasks are not particularly susceptible to the pressure to provide a socially desirable response.

Moreover, with projective tasks, the researcher must develop a means for coding responses. It is important, therefore, to carefully evaluate the validity of such measures, using the techniques described earlier.

> *The most common type of measure for assessing internal states is the use of structured scales.*

Scales

Probably the most common type of measure for assessing internal states is the use of structured scales. We have scales for assessing variables such as communication apprehension, communicator style, argumentativeness, self monitoring, and need for inclusion. Scales differ in whether they are designed to tap some enduring trait or predisposition, such as those just mentioned, or some momentary state, such as the perceived credibility of a particular speaker.

The reasons for the popularity of scales are obvious: They can be administered quickly to large groups of people, and they also can be scored quickly. Thus it is possible to secure large quantities of data with relative ease.

The reliability, validity, and utility of a set of scales obviously varies with the nature of the scales. It is not possible to say that scales in general are more valid or useful than other forms of data. Judgments must be made about each set of scales individually.

There is an entire science of scale construction that has investigated alternative formats in an attempt to determine some general properties of scales. Although it is difficult to indicate what forms of scales are most valid and useful, there are some guidelines that indicate what forms are likely to produce the most reliable or consistent results.

For instance, scales that specify what each alternative means frequently enhance reliability. Consider the format of a semantic differential scale:

kind __:__:__:__:__:__:__ cruel

Here the meaning of each alternative response is left for the subject to define. Had the seven alternatives been labeled, for instance, "extremely kind," "moderately kind," "somewhat kind," "equally kind and cruel," "somewhat cruel," "moderately cruel," and "extremely cruel," subjects might vary less in their individual interpretation.

Moreover, the reliability of a scale may be affected by the number of alternative responses from which the subject may choose. Individuals are likely to be more consistent when choosing from a relatively restricted rather than a large number of alternatives. It is therefore not surprising that a number of evaluative scales, such as credibility of a source or scales designed to measure attitudes toward an issue, are frequently restricted to seven levels of evaluation.

When the scale is intended to assess an enduring predisposition, such as communication apprehension, rather than a temporary state, the scale must be able to index the predisposition under all conditions. Here content validity, or the adequate sampling of a domain, becomes a relevant consideration.

It is not possible to identify even a small portion of the issues one considers in scale construction. With scales, as with any other measuring procedure, the researcher must either locate an existing instrument with documented reliability and validity or test the scale for these two attributes.

❏ Combining Types of Measures

As you can see, each type of measurement procedure has advantages and limitations. To compensate for the weaknesses of a single type of measuring procedure, some researchers use multiple approaches within the same study. Recall the work of Bell (1985) on the conversational involvement of lonely people. He analyzed features of their actual conversations (behavior observed directly without the subjects knowing the variables of interest), asked the subjects about their own perceptions of their conversation (self report), and had their partners indicate their perceptions of the conversation of the lonely individual (observer report). Although the three types of measures did not yield identical results, a general pattern emerged that characterized conversation of lonely individuals as passive and restrained.

❏ Study Questions

Divide into groups of four and answer the following:

1. Suppose that you are doing a study in which the dependent variable is liking of a stranger following initial interaction. Suggest the following kinds of measures and evaluate your suggestions:
   a. a measure of behavior where the individual does not know that the researcher is observing the behavior
   b. report by an observer
   c. self-report
   d. selection from preformulated behavior
2. If the individuals in the study described above knew the nature of the study, in what way might it influence the result of the study?
3. The two most common types of dependent variables in interpersonal communications are self-report scales and behavior that is coded by the researcher. Compare the general advantages and limitations of these two forms of data.

9

Describing a Data Set:
Central Tendency and Dispersion

Once data have been collected, the researcher needs to describe them in a manner that permits the type of analyses necessary to determine whether or not the hypothesis has been confirmed. Since responses may have been gathered from several hundred individuals, they cannot be reported in their entirety. Consequently, some statistics simply serve as summarizing techniques.

Such summary or descriptive statistics serve about the same purpose as the box score of a basketball game. The report of the game cannot describe each play in detail. The reporter offers a statistical summary as a shorthand way of capturing the most important features of the game.

Two of the most common summary statistics computed for a data set are a measure of central tendency and a measure of dispersion. The *central tendency* of a data set refers to a single score that typifies the entire set of scores. For example, an instructor who has given an examination may wish to identify a single score that best describes the performance of the entire class. The *dispersion* of the data set indicates the degree of variability in the set of scores. The instructor may want to know not only what the most typical score is, but also how much variability there was about this score.

Before we discuss measures of central tendency and dispersion, it is necessary to consider certain scaling properties of the data themselves. For as we shall see, the particular measure of central tendency or dispersion computed is constrained by the nature of the data. Thus in this chapter we first will discuss scaling properties of data and then describe common measures of central tendency and variability.

❏ Scaling Properties

There are underlying properties of data that constrain the way in which the data can be represented numerically. Similarly, the range of statistics that can be applied to a data set are restricted by the underlying scaling properties of the data. The researcher must, therefore, characterize the data in a manner consistent with the underlying properties of the data and likewise, choose procedures for analysis that are appropriate to the scaling properties of the data.

There are four levels of scales, each more restrictive than the next: nominal, ordinal, interval, and ratio. Thus the ratio scale possesses all the characteristics of the other three, the interval scale has all the characteristics of the nominal and ordinal scales, and the ordinal scale possesses the properties of the nominal scale.

NOMINAL SCALES

A *nominal scale*, the least restrictive, requires only that the categories to which each piece of data is assigned be discrete. There is no assumption regarding the natural ordering of the categories. Thus one category cannot be claimed to possess more or less of some variable than another, only to be unique. Suppose that we decided to categorize the statements made in a discussion in the following way: offering information, seeking information, suggesting a proposal, supporting another's position, challenging another's position, and making a procedural suggestion. These categories can be said to constitute a nominal scale. Presumably they are unique (i.e., non-overlapping). However, there is no natural order among them; in other words, they could not be ordered along some continuum representing an underlying variable.

Note that any individual case can be assigned only category membership. For instance, a particular utterance might be classified as seeking information. But no individual case could be assigned a score. It would not make sense to assign seeking information a score of "3" and offering information a score of "2". Although we cannot assign a score to an individual case, it would be possible to characterize the data set as a whole by noting how many cases fall within each category. But all that can be said about an individual case is that it falls within a particular category.

Consider a study by Cupach and Metts (1986) comparing the dissolution of relationships of married and unmarried couples. Participants were asked to describe the events leading up to and culminating in the divorce. These accounts were coded for a number of features, one of which was attempts to repair the relationship. Attempts to repair were categorized into one of four types: self effort, partner effort, mutual effort, or status quo (waiting out the situation hoping that it would resolve itself without explicit effort). As you can see, there is no natural ordering among the categories. It would not make sense to assign a higher score for using a particular category. But it is possible to determine which category was reported as used most frequently by an entire group. For instance, in married couples, the most frequent attempts at repair were categorized as self effort (47%), whereas this category was used less frequently by unmarried couples (only 22% of their attempts at repair fell in this category).

ORDINAL SCALES

Ordinal scales order discrete categories along a continuum that reflects some underlying variable, but the distance between the categories need not be constant.

For instance, a researcher might use the following scale to characterize same-sexed friendships:

strangers
casual acquaintances
casual friends
good friends
very close friends

The categories are not ordered randomly as they were with nominal data. Rather, they are ordered along a continuum from least intimate to most intimate. But no assumption is made that the distance between any two adjacent categories is the same as that between any other two adjacent categories. For example, there may not be much difference in the intimacy we feel toward casual acquaintances and casual friends. But we may consider our relationship with good friends to be much more intimate than our relationship with casual friends. Just as with nominal scales, individuals do not have a score. But individual observations can be rank ordered on a scale like the one described so that it is possible to conclude that a particular observation possesses more or less of a particular property, intimacy in this case, than another observation.

INTERVAL SCALES

Interval scales are scales that order discrete categories along a continuum reflecting some underlying variable, with the distance between adjacent intervals being constant. Thus an interval scale has the same properties as an ordinal scale, with the additional restriction that the distance between any two adjacent categories is the same as the distance between any other two adjacent categories. Suppose the researcher's interest was in the number of minutes it takes each group to reach consensus in making a decision. The number of minutes would reflect an interval scale, because the difference between 29 and 30 minutes, for instance, is exactly the same as the difference between 55 and 56 minutes.

RATIO SCALES

Ratio scales are ordered discrete categories along a continuum reflecting an underlying variable, with the distance between variables being constant and with an absolute zero. As you can see, the only difference between an interval and a ratio scale is the additional requirement for a ratio scale that there must be an absolute zero. In other words, with a ratio scale, it must be possible for there to be a true zero or a total absence of the variable being measured. The measurement of minutes required to reach consensus could not be a ratio scale, because, if consensus must be reached, there could not be a total absence of talk. By contrast however, the measure of the number of utterances by each member of the group would be a ratio scale, because it is possible for some members to make no utterances at all.

For our purposes, however, the distinction between interval and ratio scales is unimportant, because the statistics of interest to communication scholars can be applied to interval level data as well as to ratio level data. It is important to realize, though, that the higher the level of the scale, the greater the flexibility the researcher has in selecting statistics for analysis. Thus, interval data allow us to use any statistic applicable to nominal or ordinal data. The researcher must know the level of data inherent in the scale being used to select the particular statistics to be computed. In fact, the researcher may choose a particular measuring instrument initially because it will make it possible later to conduct the desired analysis.

❏ Descriptive Statistics

The nature of the research question will determine what particular features of the data set are of most interest. When the data set consists of an array of scores on a single variable, the two most common types of descriptive statistics are measures of central tendency and of dispersion. As mentioned earlier, we frequently want to know the single score that is in some way typical of all the others (reflected in a measure of central tendency) as well as how tightly clustered or varied the scores happen to be (represented by a measure of dispersion). The particular measure of central tendency and of dispersion computed is contingent on the scaling properties or level of data underlying the data set.

CENTRAL TENDENCY

Recall that a *measure of central tendency* is a single number designed to typify the "average" score for the data set. Because nominal level data do not yield an individual score for each observation, it is not possible to compute an actual average with nominal data. It is possible, however, to identify the category that has the largest membership.

Mode

The *mode* (M_o) is the category with the largest number of cases. In the example of attempts to repair relationships cited earlier (Cupach & Metz, 1986), the modal type of repair for married couples was self effort, because this was the most frequent type of repair. Some distributions are bimodal or even trimodal. In such instances, two or three categories are tied for greatest membership.

For some purposes, the mode can be a very useful statistic. Suppose, for instance, that a band director needed to order new instruments for a group of incoming students whose preferences for instruments were not yet known. The director would try to anticipate the most popular choice (i.e., the modal preference) in order to acquire the greatest number of these instruments. Similarly, the researcher characterizing the efforts of several couples to salvage their relationships may find it useful to indicate whether the dominant attempt at repairing a dissolving relationship is self effort, partner effort, mutual effort, or no overt effort.

The mode is the only measure of central tendency that can be computed with nominal data. Although other options are available when the data are ordinal or interval, the mode could also be computed for data of these levels as well.

Median

With ordinal or interval level data, it is possible to compute a measure of central tendency called a median. A *median* (X_{50}) is the point on a scale above which and below which 50% of the cases in the distribution of scores fall. Notice that the median is a point on the scale and need not coincide with any actual response. Rather, it divides the scores into two groups of equal size.

Consider, for example, an examination on which you are told that the median score is 82. This means that half the scores on the test were above 82 and half were below 82. You do not know whether anyone had the exact score of 82.

The median is a useful measure of central tendency because it is not affected by *deviant cases* (cases that are markedly different from the rest). In the example just cited, most people may have scored between 63 and 98. But there may also have been two extremely deviant cases, perhaps 13 and 20. These two deviant cases would have little effect on the median, although as we shall see shortly, they would have more effect on the arithmetic mean. The median is less useful than the arithmetic mean, however, for generalizing from a sample to a population due to the nature of the statistics that are used for such purposes.

The mean is perhaps the most common measure of central tendency reported in communication research.

Mean

With interval level data it is possible to compute the arithmetic average of a group of scores, or the *mean* ($\overline{X}$) of the distribution. Dividing the sum of scores by the number of scores produces the mean.

As just mentioned, a deviant score can have marked impact on the mean. At times, therefore, the mean may not be as close to most of the scores as the median is. The mean is particularly useful, however, when the researcher wishes to make inferences from the sample to the population. The mean is perhaps the most common measure of central tendency reported in communication research.

DISPERSION

The *dispersion* of a set of scores refers to the degree of variability of the scores. It is important to know the degree of dispersion, because if it is great, a measure of central tendency may be quite discrepant from many of the individual scores. By contrast, with a set of tightly clustered scores that have little dispersion, a measure of central tendency will be relatively close to most of the scores in the data set.

Consider, for example, two sets of final examinations, each with a mean score of 85. Suppose that one set of scores ranges from 75 to 95, whereas the other set ranges from 42 to 100.

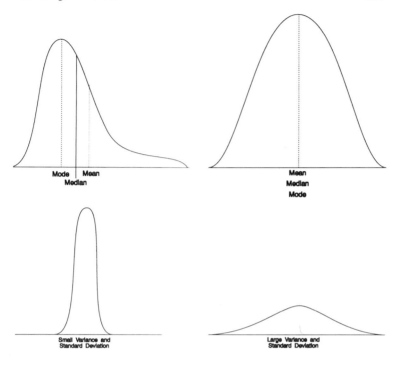

Descriptions of Data Distributions

Despite having identical means, it is easy to see that the two sets of scores are quite different from each other. In one case the mean score represents a fairly typical score in the data set, whereas in the other instance it would not be possible to identify any score as relatively typical.

Range

For purely descriptive purposes, variability may be represented by the range of scores in the data set. The *range of scores* is simply the difference between the highest true score and lowest true score. In other words, the range is computed by subtracting the smallest true score from the largest true score. The range is useful for describing the variability of a data set unless the scores on the extremities tend to be highly deviant from most of the scores in the set. In these cases, the range is much larger than it would be if these deviant scores were not part of the data set. The range is seldom included in research reports because it is not useful for generalizing from a sample to a population.

The more commonly reported measures of variability are variance and standard deviation. Unfortunately, these statistics are a bit more difficult to conceptualize than the range, but they are more useful than the range when generalizing from a sample to a population.

Variance

The *variance* (s^2) of a set of scores is the average of the squared deviation (difference) of each score from the mean. If you subtracted each score from the mean, squared this deviation, and then found the average of these squared deviations, you would have computed the variance of a set of scores. It was necessary to square the deviations from the mean because the average of the deviations (not squared) would always be zero and therefore give no indication of the variability in the scores. The greater the dispersion of a set of scores from the mean, the greater the variance.

Standard Deviation

One limitation in using variance as a measure of dispersion is that variance is always in squared units of the original scores. Thus if the original scores were a set of test scores, variance would be reported as a measure of test scores squared, which is very difficult to conceptualize.

Consequently, a related measure of dispersion is more commonly reported, specifically the standard deviation of a group of scores. The *standard deviation* of a set of scores (*s* or *s.d.*) is computed by taking the square root of the variance of that set of scores. By doing so, we once again have a measure of dispersion that is in the original unit of the scores. To continue our example, the square root of the variance scores on a final examination with a mean of 85 might be 3 (on the same scale as the examination). The smaller the standard deviation, the more tightly clustered the scores are around the mean. For instance, on the same examination, if the mean were still 85 but the standard deviation were 7, we would know that there was greater variability in the scores than if the standard deviation were 3. A research report frequently will describe a data set by indicating the mean and standard deviation of the scores.

❑ Study Questions

Divide into groups of four and discuss the following questions.

For each of the forms of data described below, determine (a) whether it reflects a nominal, ordinal, or interval scale; (b) what measures of central tendency could be computed; and (c) whether it is possible to compute variance.

1. A rater observes a group of strangers interacting and then rank orders these individuals according to their level of interpersonal communicative competence.

2. A rater observes a group of strangers interacting and then indicates whether each member of the groups is best labeled as unusually outgoing, shy, or typical.

3. A rater observes a group of strangers interacting and then rates each individual on a seven-point scale designed to measure level of interpersonal communicative competence.

4. A group of strangers interact. A transcript is made of the interaction, and for each member of the group, a coder counts the number of times that person initiated conversation with another.

5. A group of strangers interact. A transcript is made of the interaction, and a coder labels each member of the group as primarily the speaker in the conversation he or she is involved in or primarily the listener.

10

Generalizing From Sample Means to a Population

In the simplest form of an experiment, the researcher manipulates an independent variable (i.e., creates two or more conditions of that variable) and measures the impact of this manipulation on the dependent variable. Consider a study of the impact of the relationship with another (independent variable) on the reaction to a request (dependent variable) conducted by Roloff, Janiszewski, McGrath, Burns, and Manrai (1988). Actually in the study there were several dependent variables, all facets of the reaction to the request, but we will focus on only one of these, the perception of obligation to grant the request to borrow class notes.

The independent variable was manipulated by identifying the source of the request to borrow notes as a friend, an acquaintance, or a stranger (three conditions). The dependent variable was assessed by asking subjects to rate on a seven-point scale how obligated they would feel to grant the request lodged by one of these three sources.

The report of this research indicates that the greatest obligation to honor the request was felt when the source was a friend (mean of 6.10), second greatest when the source was an acquaintance (mean of 5.21), and least when the source was a stranger (mean of 3.37). If our interest were confined solely to the reactions of this particular group of subjects in this specific situation, there would be no need to do any further analyses. We can see immediately that the feeling of obligation to honor a request was greatest for a friend and least for a stranger.

Statistical significance refers to stability rather than practical importance.

But in this case, as in most communication research, we would like to know whether it is sensible to generalize beyond this particular circumstance. We want to know whether other groups of similar subjects would be likely to react similarly. In other words, we want to know whether *in general* it is reasonable to assume that individuals feel more obligation to honor the request of this type when it is initiated by a friend than by a stranger.

To determine whether a relationship observed in a particular case can be generalized to a broader population, a test of statistical significance is conducted. Put another way, a *test of significance* (or inferential statistic) indicates whether a relationship observed in a sample is unique to that particular sample or is likely to exist if the same kind of sample were drawn from a broader population. Thus significance tests refer to the stability of our results. When we conduct a test of significance, we are essentially asking whether the results are replicable. That is, we are asking whether we might expect to obtain similar results if we had used a different sample from the same population. Significance tests can be applied to a wide range of relationships observed in a sample. In this chapter we shall concentrate on generalizing differences observed in sample means to the population from which the samples were drawn.

It is important to note also that it is possible to find statistically significant or stable results that would not be significant in our everyday use of this term. In other words, it is possible to find stable results that are trivial or of little practical importance. In the illustration cited above, for instance, we might have found consistently that the mean score for obligation to a friend was 6.10 and the mean score of obligation to a stranger was 6.05. Even though this difference might be consistent and therefore replicable, the difference is probably too small to be of interest. The point to be made, then, is that statistical significance refers to stability rather than to practical importance.

Results may, of course, be both statistically significant (stable) and practically significant (i.e., not trivial but of real importance). For instance, the difference in actual means reported in the study was statistically significant and also of practical significance. But the statistical and practical significance of the results must be judged independently.

❏ Type I and Type II Errors

Tests of statistical significance involve making judgments as well as performing mathematical computations. A central judgment the researcher must make is how willing he or she is to commit the two kinds of errors that are possible when conducting a test of significance. A *Type I error* occurs when the researcher concludes that a relationship observed in a sample exists also in the population when in fact no such relationship exists in the population. A *Type II error* occurs when the researcher fails to find support for a relationship in the population that actually does exist.

In a research report, what is labeled as the *significance level* is the probability *(p)* of committing a Type I error. Suppose that you read that results were significant at the .05 level of confidence. This means that there is only a 5% chance that a Type I error has been made. In other words, only 5 times in a hundred would the researcher find sample data of the sort that occurred in this study suggesting a relationship among the variables investigated when no real relationship actually existed in the population. Thus based on results such as those observed, the researcher would be wrong only 5% of the time in concluding that a relationship existed in the population.

The significance level tells you the level of confidence you may place in the results.

A more stringent significance level, perhaps .01 or .001, means that there is an even smaller chance that a Type I error has been committed. Thus if you read that $p < .001$, this means that there is less than one chance in a thousand that results such as those observed in the sample used in the study could occur when there is no real relationship in the population. As a reader, it may be more important for you to focus on p, the significance level, than on many of the other details of the analysis, because the significance level tells you the level of confidence you may place in the results. Sometimes the significance level is labeled α, the risk of committing a Type I error.

The researcher must also be concerned about the possibility of committing a Type II error (i.e., failing to detect a real relationship that exists in the population). Thus the researcher is interested in the *power* of a statistical test, which is the likelihood of detecting a relationship that actually exists in the population.

Because the researcher wants to be able to document relationships that do exist in the population, and the power to do this is related to the probability of guarding against a Type I error, the researcher should not set a needlessly stringent level of significance. For example, the researcher probably would not set the significance level at .0001 unless there was a very good reason to do so, because this could easily lead to failing to detect a real relationship in the population.

There are additional precautions the researcher can take to enhance the power of a test of significance. The easiest of these is to have a sample of sufficient size. It is possible to compute in advance the sample size needed to detect a particular relationship.

In general it is important to balance concerns about Type I and Type II errors, because the researcher hopes to avoid making either form of incorrect judgment.

❏ Conducting Tests of Significance

Conducting any inferential or significance test should begin with the selection of the significance level. The researcher must decide what is an acceptable risk of assuming that a relationship exists in the population when, in fact, it does not (i.e., the researcher must select the probability of committing a Type I error).

Next, the researcher performs the necessary computations for the specific statistic. The numerical outcome of this computation is contingent on factors such as the number of subjects participating and the magnitude of the relationship. When conducting a significance test on sample means, the key factors are how discrepant the sample means are, how much variability exists within the sample, and how large the sample size is. Then the researcher compares the numerical result obtained from computation with that required for the level of significance designated earlier. This comparison can be made by use of tables that indicate the value of statistic necessary for significance at a given level. Most computer programs automatically indicate the significance level at which the computed result would be significant. In that case, the researcher can simply note whether the obtained significance level corresponds to the one selected earlier.

❑ Differences in Mean Scores

A commonly asked question in empirical research is whether the mean scores on a single variable differ significantly for two or more groups. For example, the researcher might compare subjects' liking of strangers (dependent variable) in two conditions that varied according to the number of statements the stranger made supporting the views of the subject during an initial interaction (independent variable). Thus, in one condition the stranger might make no supporting statements, whereas in the other condition, the stranger might issue three or more supporting statements. The difference in liking scores could be compared by a *t*-test.

t-TEST

A *t-test* is an inferential statistic to determine whether the difference observed in two sample means for the same variable indicates that a difference is likely to exist in the population means as well. Thus if a *t*-test were conducted in the illustration just cited, and the results were found to be significant, we could conclude that *in general* it seems that strangers who issue statements of support for the views of others are better liked than those who do not.

Results of a *t*-test typically include three items of information. For example

$$t (132) = 4.41, p < .05.$$

In this hypothetical illustration, $t = 4.41$ is simply the result of the numerical calculation and is the number the researcher would use when referring to the tables of significance levels. Degrees of freedom (df) are also reported, in this case, df = 132. *Degrees of freedom* are related to sample size and must also be known in order to refer to the appropriate part of the tables on significance. The significance level ($p < .05$) is the most important piece of information for the reader. Recall that the significance level reports the chance of committing a Type I error.

Therefore, in our hypothetical illustration there are fewer than 5 chances in 100 that we have concluded that supporting statements make a difference in the liking of a stranger when that is actually not the case.

A *t*-test can be computed for only one dependent variable at a time. Thus, if there is more than one dependent variable, either additional *t*-tests must be computed or some other means of accommodating the data must be used.

ONE-WAY ANALYSIS OF VARIANCE

Frequently the researcher wishes to know the influence of more than two conditions of the independent variable on the dependent variable. Think back to the illustration at the beginning of the chapter: Does the obligation to grant a request depend on the relationship with the source of the request (friend, acquaintance, or stranger)? A *one-way analysis of variance* is a procedure for determining whether the difference observed among three or more sample means are likely to exist in the population. An analysis of variance is called an *F-test*. The results are reported in a manner similar to that used for a *t*-test. In our illustration, the effect for intimacy was reported as follows:

$$F\,(2/54) = 24.9, p < .01.$$

The *F*-test is simply an extension of the *t*-test. In our illustration, the results were significant at the .01 level. So we can conclude that the obligation to grant a request does depend on the relationship one has with the person issuing the request.

A significant *F*-test tells us that the two most discrepant means (in this case the mean for friend of 6.10 and the mean for stranger of 3.37) are significantly different from each other. To determine whether the other mean (acquaintance mean of 5.21) differs significantly from either the mean for friend or for stranger, the researcher would need to perform a follow-up test, sometimes called a post host test. *Follow-up tests* are used to determine whether means other than the most extreme ones differ from any of the other means.

Just as with the t-test, a one-way analysis of variance can be performed for only one dependent variable at a time. If there are more dependent variables, then additional tests must be performed using other related procedures, such as a multivariate analysis of variance.

TWO-WAY ANALYSIS OF VARIANCE

If two or more independent variables are incorporated in the design, then the researcher must test the impact of these variables on the dependent variable. Moreover, the two variables may produce a combined effect, known as interaction, that could not have been detected if the variables had been studied separately. A *two-way analysis of variance* is a procedure for assessing the generalizability of differences observed in sample means to a broader population of two independent variables considered separately as well as in combination with each other. The impact of each independent variable on the dependent variable is called a *main effect*. The effect of the two independent variables considered in conjunction with each other is called an *interaction effect*.

Consider again whether the independent variable of relationship with the source (friend, acquaintance, or stranger) affects the obligation to grant a request (dependent variable). Suppose that the researchers had included a second independent variable, importance of the request. In one condition the request was very important (asking the individual to call an ambulance for a critically injured person) versus very unimportant (asking the individual to call the weather bureau so the individual could select appropriate clothing for the next day).

We would conduct a two-way analysis of variance in this instance because there are two independent variables. We would find an F ratio and significance level associated with the independent variable of relationship with the source, just as we did earlier ($F\ (2/54) = 24.9$, $p < .01$). We would also find an

F ratio and significance level associated with the importance of the request, perhaps $F (1/54) = 33.2$, $p < .01$. This indicates that there is a significant effect for the importance of the request. Perhaps inspection of the means would reveal that people felt a greater obligation to honor an important than an unimportant request.

There is no limit on the number of variables that can be included in an analysis of variance.

We might also have found a significant interaction between relationship with the source and importance of the request, perhaps $F (2/54) = 21.1$, $p < .05$. This tells us that the sense of obligation to honor a request is contingent on the particular combination of conditions of the two independent variables. For instance, in general, we might feel more obligation to honor the request of a friend than that of a stranger. But if the request is extremely important, we might feel an equally strong obligation to honor such a request, regardless of its source. Thus we might be quite willing to call an ambulance for a critically injured individual regardless of our relationship to this individual.

HIGHER ORDER ANALYSIS OF VARIANCE

As you might suspect, there is no theoretical limit on the number of independent variables that can be included in an analysis of variance. If the design incorporates three variables, then a three-way analysis of variance can be conducted, with three main effects, one for each independent variable. This time, however, there will be four interactions. Three of these consider the effects of combining two of the independent variables at a time. The final one indicates the combined impact of all three independent variables considered in conjunction with each other. As you can see, increasing the number of independent variables substantially increases the number of interaction effects. Although this presents no great problem, it does, at times, produce results that are complicated to interpret.

❑ Strength of Relationship

Thus far in this chapter we have focused on tests of significance, which enable the researcher to decide whether the differences in scores in the dependent variable across conditions of the independent variable can reasonably be generalized to a broader population. There is another statistic associated with these tests of significance that is of considerable importance. *Omega squared* is associated with each *t* value or each *F* value and indicates the percentage of variability in the dependent variable that can be explained by the variable that created the conditions being compared (the independent variable in an experiment).

A variety of factors are responsible for the variability observed in any dependent variability. These factors include the independent variable(s), other relevant variables, and individual variability. Omega squared indicates what percentage of the dispersion observed in a dependent variable can be attributed to the manipulation of an independent variable.

Thus in a two-way analysis of variance, the researcher would compute omega squared three times, once for each main effect and once for the interaction. In a three-way analysis of variance, omega squared would be computed for each main effect and for each of the interactions.

Consider our earlier illustration of a two-way analysis of variance. Suppose we found omega squared to be .12 for source of request, .13 for importance of the request, and .10 for the interaction. This indicates that 12% of the variation in scores of obligation felt to honor a request can be explained by the source of the request. Thirteen percent of the variation in the obligation to honor a request depends on the importance of the request. An additional 10% in the variation in the obligation to honor a request can be explained by the unique combination of the source of the request and its importance. The analysis cannot, of course, identify the additional factors that account for the remaining variability in the obligation to honor a request. The other factors might include differences between individuals in their sense of obligation as well as other variables, such as ease with which the request could be met.

The significance test tells the researcher how stable the relationship that was observed in the population is; omega squared is equally important. It indicates the strength of the relationship between the variables under observation (the independent and dependent variables in an experiment). Thus omega squared indicates whether the relationship is trivial or whether enough variation in the dependent variable can be explained to be of real interest; the larger omega squared, the greater the impact of the independent variable on the dependent variable.

❑ Interpreting Tests of Significance

Once the researcher has conducted the inferential test, it is clear whether the results are statistically significant. That is, the researcher knows whether the risk of committing a Type I error (assuming a relationship exists in the population when this is not true) is smaller than that originally selected as permissible. Thus the reader will likely encounter for each hypothesis a statement such as "The results were statistically significant," or "The results failed to reach statistical significance."

Our next concern as readers is to know how to interpret these tests of significance of differences between mean scores. Consider first the instance in which results were found to be statistically significant. It would be inaccurate to conclude that the relationship observed in the sample definitely exists in the population as well. Rather, the accurate conclusion is that the relationship observed in the sample *quite likely* exists in the population.

There are a number of reasons why a statistically significant result cannot be taken as demonstrating with total certainty that a relationship exists in the population. One of the most common of these is the possibility that a Type I error occurred. Even if the researcher selected a very conservative significance level, .001 for example, there remains the possibility that this particular sample represents the one case in one thousand in which a relationship was observed in the sample that did not also exist in the population.

Additional factors may have contributed to the relationship's occurrence in the sample when it did not exist in the population. Perhaps the relationship observed was a function of the unique conditions under which the study was performed rather than the connection among the variables themselves. For instance, many years ago, researchers reported differences in the sentence structure and vocabulary of messages that they argued were contingent upon the modality (oral versus written) in which the messages were encoded. Upon scrutiny, however, it appears that the differences were more likely a function of the extent of preparation of the message rather than the encoding modality. Written messages typically were formal, carefully prepared messages, and the oral ones were spontaneous. Thus contaminating variables, the particular instantiation of the variables, the surrounding context, and peculiarities of the sample, all are factors that could lead us to observe a relationship in the sample that does not hold for the population.

On the other hand, results that fail to reach statistical significance must be interpreted somewhat cautiously as well. We cannot conclude from results that are statistically significant that there is no relationship between the independent and dependent variables. Rather, they should be interpreted as meaning that the study *provides no evidence* for a relationship between the independent and dependent variables. For there remains the possibility that a relationship exists in the population, but this particular study failed to find evidence of this. One factor that could produce such an outcome is a Type II error. For instance, the relationship may not have been documented in the population due to insufficient sample size or large variability within the sample. Moreover, the factors cited above, such as the manner in which the variables were instantiated, surrounding conditions, and unique features of the context, could have produced results that failed to provide evidence for a relationship that actually exists in the population. For example, imagine that the researcher had hypothesized that speaker credibility affects the attitude change, but failed to find statistically significant results to support this. It may be that the hypothesis is true for non-ego-involving issues, but not for highly ego-involving ones, and the researcher used highly ego-involving issues. It would be inaccurate to conclude that no relationship exists between credibility and attitude change. The appropriate conclusion is that no evidence was found for a relationship between credibility and attitude change. This leaves open the possibility that subsequent studies (in this case ones conducted with less ego-involving issues) may provide evidence of the hypothesized relationship.

Since the results of a single study are never completely conclusive, you may wonder why researchers conduct them. There certainly is value in knowing the results of a single study. Statistically significant results provide *more* evidence than we already had to suggest a relationship in the population. And results that are not statistically significant leave us two options. Either we must revise our hypothesis, being more precise about the particular conditions under which it holds, or we must conclude that our hypothesis probably is not true.

❏ The Role of Replication

Because a single study cannot be taken as conclusive evidence that a relationship does or does not exist in the population, replication of studies becomes particularly important. If a series of studies all point to the same relationship, we have confidence in its existence.

A crucial issue concerns what should be replicated. Typically *direct replication* is defined as reproducing as closely as possible all of the specific conditions of the original study. In other words, the variables would be operationalized in the same manner, similar subjects would be used, and the same context would be duplicated as closely as possible. There is, however, good reason to replicate in a different way: remain faithful to the conceptual definitions of the variables, but use different methods of manipulating or assessing the variables, a different context, and a different kind of subjects. If the relationship observed in the original study is now replicated under dissimilar circumstances, we have considerable confidence that this is a real relationship. We would then know that the original results were not produced because of some factor unique to the conditions of that study, but actually could be observed under very different specific conditions. It would be particularly convincing to see a relationship documented in one case with the independent variable manipulated and in another case with the variable observed under naturally occurring circumstances.

❏ Study Questions

Divide into groups of four and discuss the following:

1. What is the purpose of a test of significance?
2. Give an illustration of a research question for which a Type I error would be worse than a Type II error. Give an illustration of a research question for which a Type II error would be worse than a Type I error.
3. Suppose that a *t*-test were conducted to determine the significance of differences between means for the interpersonal attractiveness of two groups of strangers as judged by observers who made ratings from a videotape showing strangers interacting. One group of strangers attempted to show interest in others and received a mean attractiveness rating of 13.2 on a 15-point scale. The other group made no special effort to show interest in others and received a mean attractiveness rating of 10.8. The *t*-test for these two means yielded the following information: t (df = 42) = 5.41, $p < .01$. A friend of yours who knows nothing about statistics reads this finding and asks what it means. What would you say?
4. In what way could the design of the study in Question 3 be altered so that the researcher would need to use a one-way analysis of

variance rather than a t-test to find the significance of the differences in the means?

5. Imagine that an additional independent variable were introduced into the design described in Question 3. One independent variable, already described, is whether the individual displays interest in others. The second independent variable is how physically attractive the individual is. One result is that individuals who are initially highly physically attractive are judged by the observers to be as attractive when they fail to display interest in others as when they do display interest in others. Is this result a main effect or an interaction? Why?

6. Suppose that someone read the results reported in Question 3 and said they still didn't believe that this would be true in all cases. Are they correct? How should these results be interpreted?

11

Describing the Association
Among Variables

So far we have focused on analyzing differences between mean scores on a single dependent variable. Suppose, however, that we have scores for the same individuals on two different variables and we want to know whether these two sets of scores are related. For example, we might have scores on a measure of communicative competency for a group of children and we might also have scores for these same children on a measure of popularity with their peers. We want to know whether communicative competency is related to popularity.

To answer a question like this one, we would use a measure of association. *Measures of association* assess the relationship between two or more variables. Many measures of association are more likely to be used in descriptive than in experimental studies. One basic difference between these statistical procedures and those discussed in the preceding chapter is that with measures of association, frequently all the scores apply to the same group of subjects rather than to different groups of subjects. Although we cannot discuss all measures of association used in communication research, we will review some of the most common ones.

❏ Pearson Product Moment Correlation

When you read about a correlation coefficient and the type is not specified, it usually refers to a Pearson product moment correlation, which is the most common statistic of association. A *Pearson product moment correlation* indicates the degree of association between two interval level variables. The question of whether communicative competency is related to popularity with peers could be answered by a Pearson product moment correlation if the researcher had scores on interval level scales for these two variables for the same group of individuals.

A Pearson product moment correlation can range in value from –1 to +1. The higher the magnitude of the correlation, the stronger the relationship. If we discovered that the correlation between communicative competency and popularity was .78, we would know that children who score high in communicative competency are likely to be very popular with other children. If the correlation had been .47, we would conclude that there was still a positive relationship between communicative competency and popularity, but that it was moderate rather than strong. And if the correlation had been .16, we would conclude that there was a weak or slight tendency for communicative competency to relate to popularity.

Correlation coefficients can be negative. For example, we might find a negative correlation, perhaps –.68, between communicative competency and communication apprehension (fear of speaking). This indicates that individuals who score high on one variable score low on the other. That is, an individual who is very competent experiences a low level of anxiety

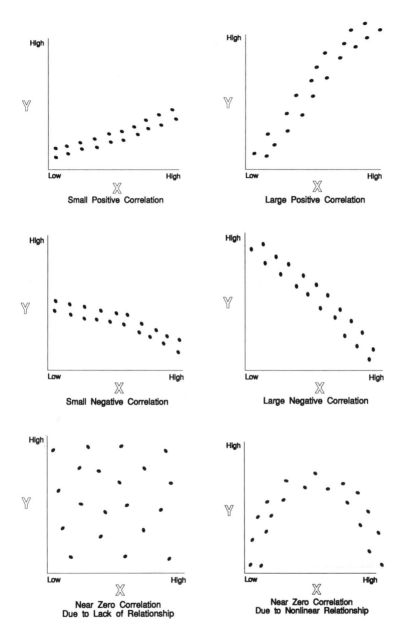

Plot of Individual Cases Showing
Possible Relationships Between the Two Variables

about speaking, whereas an individual who is low in competence experiences a high level of anxiety. How strong this relationship is depends on the magnitude of the correlation. Thus a correlation of −.82 would indicate a stronger negative relationship than a magnitude of −.21.

Once the researcher knows the strength of the relationship, stability should be considered.

The actual *strength of the relationship* between the two variables, regardless of whether the correlation is positive or negative, is indicated by squaring the correlation coefficient. Recall our earlier example in which we found a correlation of .78 between communicative competency and popularity. If we square .78, we get .61. This tells us that 61% of the variance in popularity is shared with the variance in communicative competency. With a moderate correlation between these variables of .47, squaring the correlation coefficient yields a shared variance between the two variables of 22%. And with a weak correlation of .16, only 3% of the variance is held in common by the two variables.

We would follow the same procedure if the correlation coefficient was negative. With our negative correlation between communicative competency and communication apprehension of −.68, squaring the coefficient yields a shared variance of 46%. As you can see, the amount of variance actually shared by the two variables is always smaller than the correlation coefficient, except in the rare instances where the correlation is perfect (either −1 or +1).

Once the researcher knows the strength of the relationship, stability should be considered. When we find the correlation coefficient based on a specific group of individuals, we are likely to want to know whether this is a stable or replicable finding. Just as with mean scores, we want to know whether we typically would find similar results if we had drawn a different sample of the same sort.

To answer this question about stability of the correlation, we do a significance test, once again a *t*-test. The results of the *t*-test for the significance of a correlation coefficient are reported in the same manner as t-tests for differences in means. Thus we might read that t (140) = 3.41, p < .05. This would indicate to us that fewer than 5 times in 100 would we find a correlation coefficient as large as the one we observed if no real relationship existed between the variables in the population.

A small sample size does not affect the magnitude of a correlation coefficient, but it does affect its stability. Thus even with a sample as small as 10, we might observe a relatively large correlation. But when we conducted our significance test, we might find that the correlation was not significant, suggesting that if we drew a different sample of 10, we might not find the same kind of relationship.

In interpreting measures of association, remember that they truly are measures of association and do not imply causality. Even though we may find a strong correlation between communicative competency and popularity, we cannot conclude that communicative competency caused the children to be popular. Both of these variables may result from some other underlying variable, such as concern for the needs of others. Even though we sometimes refer to one variable as the predictor and the other as the criterion variable, it is important to remember that we cannot conclude that they are causally related.

❑ Multiple Correlation

Consider the situation confronted by Sypher and Zorn (1986) in which they wanted to use communication measures to predict an individual's job level. In other words, they assumed that individuals with good communicative skills would hold better positions in a corporation than those with weaker communicative skills. They devised an index of the level of the position an individual held within the firm, designated as job level. But rather than relying on a single measure of communicative competency, they wanted to know how a variety of communication-related measures would relate to job level. They chose four measures: cognitive differentiation (the number of constructs individuals use for perceiving others), perspective-taking (how well an individual understands the views of others), self-monitoring (the extent to which individuals respond to external cues to guide their self presentation), and persuasive ability.

Sypher and Zorn obtained all five measures (the four predictor variables plus the criterion variable of job level) on a group of individuals working in a large East coast organization over a four-year period. Combining the results of the four years, inspection of the Pearson product moment correlations of each predictor variable with the criterion showed that cognitive differentiation was the most highly correlated ($r = .55$) with job level, followed by perspective-taking ability ($r = .51$), persuasive ability ($r = .50$), and self-monitoring ($r = .44$).

Therefore, if forced to predict job level from a single variable, you would choose to use cognitive differentiation. However, since you have information on the other predictor variables, it seems sensible to use this additional information as well. *Multiple correlation* is a procedure for predicting a criterion variable from two or more predictor variables. A multiple correlation is represented by an R. Just as with a Pearson product moment correlation, when you square R, you find the amount of variance in the criterion variable that is shared with the predictor variables.

Thus if we used the single best predictor of job level, by squaring the correlation of cognitive differentiation and job level (.55), we would find that 30% of the variation in job level is shared with the variation in cognitive differentiation. We want to know whether adding additional predictor variables will increase the amount of variance in the criterion variable that is shared with the predictor variable. This depends on how highly intercorrelated the predictor variables are with each other. If the remaining predictors are very highly intercorrelated with the one already used, then they add little new information in predicting our criterion variable, because they are essentially redundant. If they are lowly intercorrelated, however, they may add substantial new information. In our example, self monitoring, even though the least highly correlated with job level, added the most new information because it was not highly intercorrelated with the other predictor variables. Thus by adding self monitoring to cognitive differentiation as a predictor variable, we could raise the variance shared with job level from 30% to 41%. Adding perspective taking raised the shared variance to 47% and including persuasive ability raised the shared variance to 49%. As you can see, using the single best predictor (cognitive differentiation) accounted for less than one third of the variation in job level. By using all four predictor variables, however, you can account for almost one half the variation in job level.

As you might suspect, once a multiple correlation is computed, it should be tested for significance. The researcher should determine whether the multiple correlation observed in the sample is likely to reflect a real relationship in the population. And as with any correlation coefficient, we can never assume that predictor variables cause the criterion variable. We know only the extent to which they are related.

❑ Partial Correlation

At times the researcher may wish to investigate the relationship between two variables while holding the impact of a third (or perhaps more) variable(s) constant. Consider a study (Clark & Delia, 1977) that revealed a positive relationship between children's perspective taking ability and their ability to produce persuasive strategies adapted to the views of the persuadee ($r = .64$). Since the children in the study represented a wide age range (second through ninth graders), the correlation may have reflected the fact that most children get better at both perspective taking and persuasive argument as they get older.

Thus it is possible that there is no real relationship between perspective taking and listener adapted strategies.

To test this possibility, the researchers used a partial correlation. A *partial correlation* indicates the relationship between two variables while holding the impact of one or more additional variables constant. In this case, the partial correlation indicated the relationship between perspective taking and listener adapted arguments while holding the impact of age constant. In other words, the relationship between perspective taking and listener adapted arguments was computed *as though* all of the children had been of the same age. The partial correlation holding age constant was .51. This result indicated that there is a real relationship between perspective taking and listener adapted arguments, even when the effect of age is held constant. Once again, the researcher would need to test a partial correlation for significance.

❏ Spearman Rank Order Correlation

All of the preceding statistics require interval level data. If the data available are ordinal level rather than interval level, the research can compute a rank order correlation. Probably the most common of these is the *Spearman rank order correlation*, which indicates the degree of association between two ordinal level variables. It yields a value from –1 to +1, is interpreted in the same manner as a Pearson product moment correlation, and is tested for significance in much the same way.

❏ Chi Square

At times the data are nominal level; that is, responses can be divided into categories but not ordered or scored. Consider a study of the responses of children who wish to reject the pressure of a peer to smoke (Reardon, Sussman, & Flay, 1989). Most of the children's responses fell into five categories: simple rejection ("No"), statement of behavior ("I don't smoke"), statement of attitude ("I don't want to smoke"), rejection of other ("Get away from me"), and walk away (I'd walk away). The researchers wanted to determine whether situational variables affected the choice of the particular strategy used. For instance, they wanted to know whether the response chosen depended on the relationship with the person exerting pressure (friend or acquaintance).

To test whether responses are more likely to fall in one category than another, a statistic called chi square can be used. *Chi square* is a significance test used to determine whether the actual frequency of occurrence of responses in a particular set of categories differs from what might be expected. In our example, the researchers wanted to know whether the categories of response used most frequently with a friend were also those used most frequently with an acquaintance. The chi-square analysis indicated that this was not the case; simple rejection was used more frequently with friends than with acquaintances. Just as with other tests of significance, from the standpoint of the consumer the most important information reported is the significance level. In this instance, $p < .0001$ suggests that the results were not a function of the particular sample but likely would be replicated with a different sample. In this case, then, we can say that there is a relationship between the kind of refusal a child will issue and the relationship with the person exerting the pressure to smoke.

With data like these it would also be possible to compute a *contingency coefficient*, which indicates the strength of the relationship between the two nominal level variables. A contingency coefficient ranges from 0 to 1 and is interpreted much like a Pearson product moment correlation (with the exception that it is not likely to approach 1 closely). Thus a larger contingency coefficient suggests a stronger relationship between the variables.

With the exception of chi square, the statistics we have discussed in this chapter differ from those discussed in the preceding chapter in the sequence in which analyses are performed. When investigating differences in means, the researcher first performs the significance test (t-test or analysis of variance) and then assesses the strength of the relationship. For correlational procedures, the researcher begins by computing the strength of the relationship and then determines whether it is significant (through use of a t-test).

❏ Factor Analysis

At times in descriptive research the central question is not whether two variables are related, but rather whether a large number of interrelated variables can actually be reduced to a smaller number of relatively discrete groups of variables. An example may help to clarify. Rubin, Perse, and Barbato (1988) were interested in identifying people's underlying motives for engaging in interpersonal communication. They asked people to rate their agreement on a 5-point scale with statements that began "I talk to people . . ." and were completed with one of 59 motives (e.g., "because it's fun," "because I'm concerned about them," and "because I want someone to do something for me.").

These researchers assumed that individuals don't really have 59 different motives for communicating. It seemed reasonable that many of these items would cluster together and could thus be reduced to a smaller number of underlying motives. Consequently, they used a procedure called *factor analysis*, which reduces a large number of original variables to a smaller number of underlying factors that reflect the relatively discrete characteristics represented in the original data.

Factor analysis is conducted by intercorrelating all the variables in the original data set and using procedures for grouping together the original variables that are highly intercorrelated. Each group of original variables is called a factor. It is labeled

FACTOR I	friendly	talkative	vivacious	considerate	kind	helpful
friendly	—	.84	.77	.42	.47	.33
talkative	.84	—	.93	.26	.18	.16
vivacious	.77	.93	—	.27	.19	.17
considerate	.42	.26	.27	—	.91	.82
kind	.47	.18	.19	.91	—	.86
helpful	.33	.16	.17	.82	.86	—

FACTOR II

A Hypothetical Intercorrelation Matrix Used in
a Factor Analysis of Personality Traits

by determining what all the original variables in the group have in common. In our example, factor analysis yielded six factors or underlying motives for interpersonal communication: pleasure, affection, inclusion, escape, relaxation, and control. For instance, the original variables that grouped together to constitute the factor of pleasure included statements such as "talking is fun," "talking is exciting," "talking is thrilling," and "talking is entertaining" from the original list of 59 motives. As you can see, the primary purpose is to take a large number of variables thought to be interrelated and to reduce them to a smaller set of factors that are not highly related.

Unlike all of the other statistics we have discussed so far, there is no single procedure for conducting factor analysis that guarantees that all researchers working with the same data set will reach the same conclusion. A number of judgments are required. For instance, the researcher must decide whether it is necessary for the factors extracted to be completely independent of each other, and the researcher must decide how closely the newly identified factors must be related to the original variables. Consequently there is no single factor analysis that can be computed for a specific data set. It is possible to compare factor analyses computed on the same set of original variables to see whether they differ significantly from each other.

❏ Study Questions

Divide into groups of four and discuss the following:

1. Suppose you read a paper that reports that there is a correlation of .43 between the number of times a person smiles during a conversation and the rating of friendliness that person received from an observer viewing a videotape of the conversation. What does that correlation mean?

2. Suppose you find that there is a correlation of –.76 between the number of times an individual interrupts others and ratings of politeness made by observers viewing individuals interacting with others. What does this correlation mean?

3. Suppose there is a correlation of .43 between the number of times a person smiles and ratings of friendliness and a correlation of .32 between the number of times an individual expresses direct interest in what the other is saying and ratings of friendliness. What additional information do you need to make an estimate of the multiple correlation of ratings of friendliness with both smiles and statements of interest as predictors?

4. Imagine that there is a correlation of .45 between number of hours studied for a test and the grade on the test. Suppose that you were able to partial out of this correlation the effect of intelligence of the test taker. Would you expect the partial correlation to be higher or lower than .45? Why?

5. You find a chi square between gender of a speaker and judgments of whether the person is more likely to offer or seek opinions in a conversation that is significant at the .05 level. What does this mean?

6. You read that a group of 23 nonverbal measures of individuals' interactions were factor analyzed and two factors were found: one was characterized as gregariousness and the other as supportiveness. What does this mean with respect to the original 23 measures?

12

Reporting the Study

The way a study is reported will depend on the purpose of the report. At times reports are intended to give a nonexpert audience a general sense of what was done, either centered on the specific study or as part of a program of research in the same area. If you read publications designed for a lay audience, such as *Psychology Today* or *Scientific American*, you will find such reports.

The kind of report we will focus on is designed for fellow researchers. In other words, we will consider the kind of report you would encounter in a professional journal such as *Human Communication Research* or *Communication Monographs*. The guideline that the writer should follow when reporting for fellow researchers is being sufficiently precise and detailed that another researcher could replicate the study. This level of precision in reporting also enables fellow researchers to evaluate both the internal and external validity of the study. In this chapter we will describe the four major sections of a typical report of empirical research: introduction, methods, results, and discussion.

❏ Introduction

The primary function of the introduction (sometimes called "background" is to identify the importance and general purpose of the study. To do so, the researcher must (1) specify the hypotheses or research questions and (2) justify their significance.

Justification of the significance of a research question may require providing an argument for the value of the general line of research as well as for the unique contribution the particular study makes to this area of research. To accomplish these ends, the researcher uses other research to construct arguments concerning the value of pursuing specific questions. The introduction does not summarize all of relevant research known to the investigator, rather, it provides the basis for justifying the particular question at issue.

The researcher must also clearly identify the question(s) to be pursued. Thus key variables should be defined conceptually. At times the researcher will also justify in the introduction the selection of the particular operational definitions of the variables to be used.

By the end of the introduction, the overall design of the study should be evident. That is, the consumer should know what the independent variables are, what levels of each variable are involved, and the nature of the dependent variables. At the end of the introduction the reader should understand the significance of the project and the specific questions or hypotheses to be pursued.

❑ Methods

As the label for this section implies, the function of this section is to describe what the researcher actually did from the time the research question was identified until data were analyzed. At times subsections, such as "subjects," "materials," and "procedures," will be used.

SUBJECTS

In the section designated as "subjects," the researcher describes the general characteristics of the subjects, how they were selected, and how they were assigned to specific experimental conditions if the study is an experiment. The characteristics of the subjects reported may bear some relationship to the variables under investigation. Frequently age, sex, and social or educational status are reported.

MATERIALS

The section designated as "materials" provides a description of manipulations, measuring instruments, or other items selected or developed for the study. Suppose, for instance, the researcher needed alternative versions of a message to manipulate the variable of assertiveness of the speaker. The materials section quite likely would contain a description of how the message was altered for each condition, and perhaps results of a pre-test indicating that the manipulation had been successful. Similarly, this section would be likely to describe the measures used, along with evidence of their reliability and validity.

PROCEDURES

The section called "procedures" provides a sequential description of what subjects in the main study did. Typically the researcher indicates what instructions subjects received, what tasks they performed, and the conditions under which they performed these tasks.

CODING THE DATA

Depending on the nature of the measures used for assessing the dependent variable(s), a fourth section may be included, specifically, "coding the data." This is necessary when responses cannot be directly converted to numerical form. In this section the researcher describes how the data were categorized or interpreted. The documentation for the reliability and validity of the procedure should be included.

ANALYSIS OF DATA

Finally, the researcher may include a section labeled "analysis of data." This describes the statistical procedures used to answer the research questions.

By the end of the methods section the reader should know exactly what happened when the study was conducted.

❑ Results

The function of this section is to report the analysis of the data in such a manner that the reader knows the degree of support (or lack of support) found for the research questions of hypotheses. Frequently the analysis of data will yield additional information as well. It therefore becomes the responsibility of the researcher to devise a way of reporting the information so that the reader knows how much confidence to place in the hypotheses or relationships under investigation.

In this section, the researcher should not interpret the results, but rather simply describe them. The researcher may, of course, report results in addition to those that bear directly on the hypothesis if they provide useful information.

By the end of the results section the reader should know whether the hypotheses were confirmed or what the answer was to the research question.

❑ Discussion

The function of the final section is to interpret the significance of the results (i.e., not their statistical significance, but the importance that should be attached to them). In this section the researcher typically considers a number of factors. For instance, the researcher should identify any limitations to either the internal or external validity of the design that may influence the manner in which the reader interprets the results. The researcher should also reflect upon the way in which the results of this study extend the line of research from which it derives. Thus consistencies should be noted and inconsistencies interpreted. The manner in which the results of the present study facilitate our thinking about the area should be identified. And at times, it is appropriate for the researcher to suggest specific directions that extensions of the present work might take. At the end of the discussion section, the reader should understand what contribution has been made by the study.

❑ Study Questions

Find an empirical research report in an area of interest to you and respond to the following questions:

1. Does the introduction adequately justify the general area of inquiry and the specific contribution to be made by this study?
2. Are the specific research question (or hypothesis) and variables involved in the study clearly identified in the introduction?

3. Is it easy to understand the exact procedures followed by the participants?
4. Are the operational definitions of all variables clear?
5. From the results section can you tell whether the hypothesis was confirmed or what the answer was to the research question?
6. Does the discussion section (a) identify any limitations of the study, (b) interpret the significance of the results, and (c) indicate how the results of this study clarify or extend thinking on the issue in question?

References

Baxter, L. A., & Bullis, C. (1986). Turning points in developing romantic relationships. *Human Communication Research, 12,* 469-493.

Bearison, D. J., & Gass, S. T. (1979). Hypothetical and practical reasoning: Children's persuasive appeals in different social contexts. *Child Development, 50,* 901-903.

Bell, R. A. (1985). Conversational involvement and loneliness. *Communication Monographs, 52,* 218-235.

Berlo, D. K., Lemert, J. B., & Mertz, R. J. (1969-1970). Dimensions for the acceptability of message sources. *Public Opinion Quarterly, 33,* 573-576.

Burgoon, J. K., & Aho, L. (1982). Three field experiments on the effects of violations of conversational distance. *Communication Monographs, 49,* 71-88.

Burke, J. A., & Clark, R. A. (1982). An assessment of methodological options for investigating the development of persuasive skills across childhood. *Central States Speech Journal, 33,* 437-445.

Canary, D. J., & Spitzberg, B. H. (1987). Appropriateness and effectiveness perceptions of conflict strategies. *Human Communication Research, 14,* 93-118.

Clark, R. A. (1979). The impact of self interest and desire for liking on the selection of communicative strategies. *Communication Monographs, 46,* 257-273.

Clark, R. A., & Delia, J. G. (1977). Cognitive complexity, social perspective-taking, and functional persuasive skills in second- to ninth-grade children. *Human Communication Research, 3,* 128-134.

159

Clark, R. A., & Delia, J. G. (1976). The development of functional persuasive skills in childhood and early adolescence. *Child Development, 47*, 1008-1014.

Cupach, W. R., & Metts, S. (1986). Accounts of relational dissolution: A comparison of marital and non-marital relationships. *Communication Monographs, 53*, 311-334.

Dovidio, J. F., Brown, C. E., Heltman, K., Ellyson, L. S., & Keating, C. F. (1988). Power displays between women and men in discussions of gender-linked tasks: A multichannel study. *Journal of Personality and Social Psychology, 55*, 580-587.

Jackson, S., & Jacobs, S. (1983). Generalizing about messages: Suggestions for design and analysis of experiments. *Human Communication Research, 9*, 169-191.

Kelly, C., Huston, T. L., & Cate, R. M. (1985). Premarital relationship correlates of the erosion of satisfaction in marriage. *Journal of Social and Personal Relationships, 2*, 167-178.

McCroskey, J. C. (1966). Scales for the measurement of ethos. *Speech Monographs, 33*, 65-72.

Marwell, G., & Schmitt, D. R. (1967). Dimensions of compliance gaining behavior: An empirical analysis. *Sociometry, 30*, 350-364.

O'Keefe, B. J. (1988). The logic of message design: Individual differences in reasoning about communication. *Communication Monographs, 55*, 80-103.

O'Keefe, D. J., & Sypher, H. E. (1981). Cognitive complexity measures and the relationship of cognitive complexity to communication. *Human Communication Research, 8*, 72-92.

Reardon, K. K., Sussman, S., & Flay, B. R. (1989) Are we marketing the right message: Can kids "just say 'no' " to smoking? *Communication Monographs, 56*, 307-324.

Roloff, M. E., Janiszewski, C. A., McGrath, M. A., Burns, C. S., & Manrai, L. A. (1988). Acquiring resources for intimates: When obligation substitutes for persuasion. *Human Communication Research, 14*, 364-396.

Rubin, R. R., Perse, E. M., & Barbato, C. A. (1988). Conceptualization and measurement of interpersonal communication motives. *Human Communication Research, 14*, 602-628.

Schacter, S. (1974). *Obese humans and rats*. New York: Halstead Press.

Shaffer, D. R., & Ogden, J. K. (1988). On sex differences in self-disclosure during the acquaintance process: The role of anticipated future interaction. *Journal of Personality and Social Psychology, 51*, 92-101.

Sillars, A. L., Weisberg, J., Burgraf, C. A., & Wilson, E. A. (1987). Content themes in marital communication. *Human Communication Research, 13*, 495-528.

Sugimoto, N. (1990). A Japan-U.S. comparison of evaluations of alternative accounts for success and failure. Paper presented at the seventh annual International and Intercultural Communication Conference, Miami, FL.

Sypher, B. D., & Zorn, T. E., Jr. (1986). Communication-related abilities and upward mobility: A longitudinal investigation. *Human Communication Research, 12*, 420-431.

Thomas, S. H. (1969). Effects of monotonous delivery on intelligibility. *Speech Monographs, 36*, 110-113.

Weber, S. J., & Cook, T. D. (1972). Subject effects in laboratory research: An examination of subject roles, demand characteristics, and valid inference. *Psychological Bulletin, 77*, 273-295.

Willihngang, S. (1988). Impact of individual differences in social cognition and message strategy use on perceptions of social support and job satisfaction in nurses. Unpublished doctoral dissertation, University of Illinois, Urbana.

Witteman, H. (1988). Interpersonal problem solving: Problem conceptualization and communication use. *Communication Monographs, 55*, 336-359.

Index

About the Author

Ruth Anne Clark (Ph.D., University of Wisconsin) has taught for the past two decades at the University of Illinois, where she is Professor of Speech Communication. Her work has centered on the functional analysis of messages with an emphasis on persuasive strategies as represented in her book, *Persuasive Messages*. Professor Clark's interest in research methodology has led her to serve as an associate editor for a number of journals within the field of speech communication, including *Communication Monographs, Communication Education,* and *Communication Studies*.

NOTES

NOTES

NOTES

NOTES